The Canadian Battlefields in Italy: Sicily & Southern Italy

Eric McGeer
Terry Copp

Series Editor: Terry Copp
Design and Layout: Matt Symes

Laurier Centre for Military Strategic and Disarmament Studies
Canadian Battlefields Foundation
© 2008

Biographies:

Eric McGeer teaches Latin and history at St. Clement's School in Toronto. He holds a Ph.D. in history from the Université de Montréal and is the author of two books and several articles dealing with warfare and law in mediaeval Byzantium. His most recent publication is *Words of Valediction and Remembrance: Canadian Epitaphs of the Second World War*, Vanwell Publishing Limited: St. Catharines, 2007.

Matt Symes holds a Bachelor of Arts (History) and a Bachelor of Education from the University of New Brunswick and Masters of Arts (History) from Wilfrid Laurier University. He is an Alumnus of the 2006 Canadian Battlefields Foundation tour and is currently completing his Doctorate at Wilfrid Laurier University.

Terry Copp is Director of the Laurier Centre for Military Strategic and Disarmament Studies and Professor Emeritus at Wilfrid Laurier University. He is the author or co-author of 14 books and many articles on the Canadian role in the Second World War including travel guides to the Canadian battlefields. One of his recent books, *Fields of Fire: The Canadians in Normandy* (University of Toronto Press), won the 2004 Distinguished Book Award for non-US history from the American Society for Military History.

The Canadian Battlefields in Italy: Sicily and Southern Italy

Copyright © 2008 by the Laurier Centre for Military, Strategic and Disarmament Studies (LCMSDS) All Rights reserved. No part of this publication may be reproduced or transmitted in any form or by any means, electronic or mechanical, including photocopying, recording, or any information and retrieval system, without permission in writing from the publisher

First published in 2008 by the Laurier Centre for Military, Strategic and Disarmament Studies, Wilfrid Laurier University, Waterloo, Ontario, N2L 3C5, Canada

Printed and bound in Canada

Library and Archives Canada Cataloguing in Publication

McGeer, Eric, 1955-
   The Canadian battlefields in Italy : Sicily & Southern Italy / Eric McGeer, Terry Copp ; series editor: Terry Copp; design and layout: Matt Symes.

Includes index. Co-publishers: Canadian Battlefields Foundation.ISBN 978-0-9783441-5-3

   1. World War, 1939-1945--Battlefields--Italy--Guidebooks. 2. World War, 1939-1945--Campaigns--Sicily. 3. World War, 1939-1945--Campaigns--Italy, Southern. 4. Canada. Canadian Army--History--World War, 1939-1945. I. Copp, Terry, 1938- II. Laurier Centre for Military, Strategic and Disarmament Studies III. Canadian Battlefields Foundation IV. Title.

D763.I8M384 2008   940.54'2157   C2008-907294-4

Cover: William Ogilvie, *Field Artillery taking up positions* [CWM 19710261-4534]
Photo p. 5 [PA 163670]
Photo p. 13 [e008300274]
Photo p. 45 [e008300290]
Photo p. 71 [e008300306]

Photo p. 75 [PA 129774]
Photo p. 89 [PA 141867]
Photo p. 99 [PA 136669]
All modern photos not credited were taken by Eric McGeer with alterations by Matt Symes

Table of Contents

Sicily

Introduction

History

The Tour

Southern Italy

Introduction

History

The Tour

Additional Information

Preface

The Canadian Battlefields in Italy series began *in medias res* with the publication in 2007 of our guidebook covering the battles at Ortona and in the Liri Valley. The guidebook offered here returns to the beginning of the Italian Campaign and escorts the reader along 1st Canadian Division's path from the landing beaches in Sicily, through the island's rugged interior, and across the Strait of Messina into the strangely beautiful landscape of Southern Italy. It aims to provide Canadians interested in this chapter of our history with a concise account of the campaigns in Sicily and Southern Italy, followed by itineraries enabling them to retrace the course of events from the perspective not just of the commanders who planned each operation but of the young volunteers who faced the challenges and risks inherent in battle to carry out the tasks assigned to them. Anyone who has gone over the battlefields of northwestern Europe will be struck at once by the factors of terrain and climate that set the experience of the Canadian soldier in Sicily and Italy well apart from that of his predecessors in the Great War and of his comrades who fought their way from the Normandy beaches to the Rhineland.

In preparing this guidebook we have made a special effort to include photographs and war art not published before. The collections in the National Archives house whole series of negatives that have never been fully exploited for the record they preserve of Canada's first major land campaign of the Second World War. One particularly interesting group dates from the summer of 1944 when Sergeant J.E. DeGuire of the Canadian Army Film and Photo Unit returned to Sicily to photograph the places where the Canadians had fought the year before. A selection of these poignant shots, as well as a number of hitherto unpublished 1943 photos depicting scenes from the campaigns, are presented in this guidebook (marked by the e008300… numbers) to allow readers to envision the setting and the human drama of events now more than sixty years in the past. We have also chosen lesser known works by the war artists William Ogilvie and Charles Comfort which distil the multifaceted activity of the campaign into a series of vignettes forming an evocative visual narrative of their own. As rich in word as it is in image, the Italian Campaign also generated a remarkable dossier of regimental histories, memoirs, and secondary works that readers wishing to learn more of the Canadian experience in Italy will find in the bibliography.

It was originally our intention to publish a guidebook to Sicily only, and readers will note that by far the larger part of this guide is devoted to the Sicily campaign. The decision to append a short section covering the campaign in Southern Italy reflects our wish to make *The Canadian Battlefields in Italy* as comprehensive as possible, as well as to emphasize the importance of this somewhat neglected phase of the Italian Campaign. Although, apart from the Anglo-American landings at Salerno, there was little heavy fighting in southern Italy, the strategic choices made by both sides in the fall of 1943 set the course and character of the war in Italy. I would therefore like to express my thanks to Professor Terry Copp for contributing a historical overview supplemented by practicable itineraries which meet the needs of Canadian travellers embarking on the admittedly difficult, but often rewarding, trek from the toe of Italy to the bluffs overlooking the Sangro River.

Warm thanks are likewise due to the people who aided in assembling the material for this guidebook. Ellyse Rupert and her fellow staff at the National Archives of Canada deserve special mention for their help in acquainting me with the collections and processing my requests for photos, as do Susan Ross and the staff at the Canadian War Museum for their courteous assistance in obtaining reproductions of war art and granting permission to publish them. Lee Windsor answered several questions and provided advice at several points, while Terry Copp offered helpful comments in his review of the Sicily section. The thanks I owe to both extend in even larger measure to my colleague Matt Symes who once again displayed his expertise and sound judgment in designing the text, arranging the illustrations (including several of his own photos), and preparing the maps. I look forward to continuing our collaboration as we turn to our forthcoming guidebook on the Gothic Line and the Battle of the Rivers. A final thanks goes to Bob Hall for proofreading the manuscript.

I wish to end this preface with a dedication to the Canadians who fought in Sicily and Italy that at the same time addresses what I see as an unfortunate tendency in my own profession. As a teacher at the secondary school level, I am increasingly dismayed by the pejorative view of Canada's past promoted in the textbooks assigned in Canadian history courses. The condemnations and selectively distorted depiction of another time are especially pronounced in the sections dealing with the Second World War, which magnify the mistakes or imperfections of a generation markedly different from our own in its shaping influences, expectations, and beliefs, without according commensurate acknowledgment of the sacrifices and achievements of the Canadians who coped with the Depression, contributed far more than their fair share to the Allied war effort, and laid the foundations of the country we inhabit today. *"In the prime of life I left this world, my beloved wife and dear little girl,"* states the inscription on the headstone of Corporal Joseph Norton, killed in Sicily at age 23, one of thousands of reminders of the respect we owe to the memory of the fallen and the suffering of their families. Not far from Corporal Norton's grave in the Agira Canadian War Cemetery lies Private Steve Slavik, a young man of Czech origin whose epitaph, translated from his native tongue, reads *"Born in a foreign land, in a foreign land he lay down his young life for democracy."* Perhaps it is worth asking why these young men chose to fight for a country as flawed and xenophobic as current textbooks portray it; and why today's students are so poorly served by texts that deny just and fair recognition to a generation that gave so much in the struggle to preserve a world worth living in.

Eric McGeer

emcgeer@scs.on.ca

Introduction

Sicily

If June 6 1944 stands out as one of the most famous days in history, July 10 1943 now seems just another day in the course of a long war. Yet at the time the invasion of Sicily confirmed the change of momentum in the Second World War. Nearly four years into the war, after a litany of defeat and desperate defence, the Allies were at last carrying the fight directly to the enemy. The Anglo-American triumph in North Africa in May of 1943 meant that Hitler could no longer extend the war beyond Europe or threaten British interests in the Mediterranean. Nor any longer could the Axis powers keep the war at a distance from their populations and industrial bases. The landings in Sicily kicked the struts out from under the tottering regime of Benito Mussolini; they also coincided with the last German offensive of the war on the Eastern Front. The loss of Sicily and the failure of their titanic effort at Kursk put the Germans permanently on the defensive at a time when the escalation of the Allied bombing campaign and the shift in the Battle of the Atlantic were curtailing their strategic options. Steadily, inexorably, the Allies forced the enemy into an unwinnable contest of means, materiel, and manpower.

Seen against this broad canvas, the invasion of Sicily claims a place among the pivotal events of the war. It retains a particular significance for Canadians who, despite the abundance of narratives in word and image of the Italian campaign, remain largely unaware of their countrymen's role in what proved to be the longest Allied land campaign in western Europe. Halfway through 1943, the Canadian army, nourished on tales of its Great War predecessors and hailed as "a dagger pointed at the heart of Berlin," had little to show for itself beyond a brief round trip to the continent in 1940, the loss of two battalions at Hong Kong in 1941, and a dreadful morning at Dieppe in 1942. So it was with a sense of renewed purpose that Canadians received Mackenzie King's announcement that "armed forces of Britain, the United States and Canada are now in the forefront of an attack which has as its ultimate objective the unconditional surrender of Italy and Germany. All Canada will be justifiably proud to know that units of the Canadian Army are a part of the Allied force engaged in this attack…".

William Ogilvie, *Prelude to Invasion* [CWM 19710261-4689].

Well might all Canada take pride in its contribution. The Canadian contingent included men from every part of the country – 1st Infantry Brigade from Toronto and rural Ontario, 2nd Brigade from the western provinces, 3rd Brigade from Quebec and the Maritimes, as well as tank regiments from Quebec, Ontario, and Alberta. In the 38-day campaign that followed, the infantrymen, tank crews, artillerymen, and engineers drawn from all walks of civilian life achieved some of the most remarkable feats of arms in Canadian military history. Any Canadian who stands by the road into Leonforte, at the foot of the cliff at Assoro, or among the jagged approaches to Agira and the Salso Valley beyond cannot help but admire the fortitude of the young men who fought in the heat and dust of a Sicilian summer against a wily, seasoned enemy.

The routes laid out in this book follow 1st Canadian Division from Piazza Armerina to Adrano. Although this itinerary passes over the week between the landings and the first real baptism of fire at Valguarnera, it does save time and effort better spent on the principal events of the Canadian campaign. The narrative summarises the advance from the landing beaches southwest of Pachino to Piazza Armerina and suggests points of interest in a provisional tour for those intending to visit southeastern Sicily. The roads are good, and the towns and countryside can be quite scenic, but it is a long way to go just to retrace a march interrupted by brief delaying actions. The main tour is divided into four itineraries. The first two are fairly detailed, the final two less so, but they cover more ground. Each itinerary may require 2-3 hours at most, and the entire tour can be done in a day or two, depending on your level of interest.

In all likelihood, a Canadian battlefield tour will be part of a broader trip covering the rich classical and mediaeval heritage of Sicily. The tour therefore begins and ends near other significant sites. Basic information about travel in Sicily is given at the end of this guidebook, but for the purposes of a battlefield tour two hotels make convenient bases. The **Hotel Mosaici da Battiato**, three kilometres west of Piazza Armerina, is within walking distance of the splendid mosaics in the Roman Villa della Casale, and offers easy access to the SS 117b that leads north to Valguarnera and the Dittaino Valley. The routes through the final stages of the campaign converge around the **Hotel Castel Miralago**, located on the SS 121 two kilometres west of Regalbuto, which puts you within reach of Mount Etna and the roads through eastern Sicily. Both are reasonably priced and have good dining rooms.

In planning a visit to Sicily, keep a few things in mind. If suffocating heat, dust, haze, sunstroke, insect bites, and the odd scorpion or viper constitute the ingredients of an ideal vacation, summer is definitely the time to go. If you can do without these, a trip in March offers the compensation of cooler weather, clearer air, and the overall comfort of mind and body. Even January can be pleasant, and if you find yourself gazing over a Canadian battleground at sunset on a winter evening, the interplay of colour, light, and shadow will imprint the scene indelibly into your memory. There are superb vantage points along the way where a pair of binoculars would be useful, and you should bring along one or both of Farley Mowat's books, *The Regiment* and *And No Birds Sang*. His firsthand account of the climb at Assoro will enrich your visit to the most awe-inspiring stop on the tour.

The rugged, empty, and hauntingly beautiful landscape south of Agira (right).

Some further words of advice. It is wise to learn some Italian phrases, since English is not widely spoken in the parts of Sicily where you will be. Sicilians are courteous and helpful to foreigners who seek their assistance, all the more so to those who make the effort to speak their language. You will also have to rent a small, roadworthy vehicle. The streets in Sicilian towns could double as bowling alleys in North America, and the roads are not always in good condition, especially in spring and fall when flooding can wash out whole stretches. The tours laid out here will note the state of the roads, but this is an ever changing situation. Stay alert when driving in remote areas (hug the right side of the road on curves), and keep an eye out for signs warning about a "strada dissestata" or "strada chiusa al transito" – in other words, an unmaintained road or a road closed to traffic.

Hairpin turns on the long climb up to the citadel of Enna [Matt Symes].

Background

"Before Alamein we never had a victory; after Alamein, we never had a defeat." Even if Churchill simplified for effect, his pronouncement in *The Hinge of Fate* signalled a decisive turn of events in the war. On November 8 1942, four days after the Eighth Army restored the reputation of British arms by driving the German-Italian Panzerarmee out of Egypt, thousands of American soldiers served notice of their country's growing role in the Allied war effort as they poured onto the shores of North Africa. In the first of the large-scale operations undertaken by the

Anglo-American forces, and the first of six D-Days in the Mediterranean theatre, Operation Torch brought British and American armies to Morocco and Algeria where they proceeded to act as the second arm of the pincers closing in on the Axis forces. Three months after losing a quarter of a million men at Stalingrad, Hitler was forced to absorb the even greater loss of 275,000 Axis soldiers (100,000 of them German) in Tunisia. This number included the Luftwaffe and Wehrmacht units that the Führer had transferred from the Eastern Front to shore up his sagging Italian ally. Ironically, he might have prolonged the existence of Fascist Italy had he withheld them for subsequent operations. If the reinforcements squandered in Tunisia had been available for the defence of Sicily, the Allies would not have invaded the island.

The site of the Canadian landings near Pachino, photographed in 1944 [e008300287].

Assured of victory in North Africa, Churchill and Roosevelt met at Casablanca in January 1943 to weigh strategic options. The British and American Chiefs of Staff debated the merits of continuing operations in the Mediterranean or concentrating Anglo-American resources for a cross-Channel assault in 1943. Expressing the American view, General George Marshall argued against further efforts in the Mediterranean as a waste of resources better used in the primary confrontation with Nazi Germany. He saw no point in employing Americans to serve what he considered British imperial interests in a secondary theatre. But the arguments advanced by the British prevailed. An attack on Sicily would force the Germans to divert men and materiel not just to Italy but to Greece and the Balkans; it might well knock Italy out of the war while attracting neutral Turkey to the Allied side; and it would clear the Mediterranean for merchant shipping. Furthermore, the men and equipment required already lay to hand. Since neither the British nor the Americans truly believed that their armies were ready to take on the Germans in northwest Europe in 1943, invading Sicily offered the best opportunity to keep the large forces in the Mediterranean engaged while preparations for a cross-Channel assault in 1944 continued. The Americans reluctantly agreed to the invasion of Sicily; but what they saw as the last phase of the North African campaign, the British saw as a stepping-stone to further operations against the "soft underbelly" of the Reich.

The directive sent to General Dwight D. Eisenhower (then Commander in Chief of the Allied forces in North Africa) advised him that "the Combined Chiefs of Staff have resolved that an attack against Sicily will be launched in 1943, with the target date as the favourable July moon (Code designation 'Husky')". Planning commenced at once, but with the relevant air, naval, and land commanders still occupied in Tunisia, the assault plan was not hammered into shape until May. Even in its modified final version "Husky" was the greatest combined operation ever undertaken, surpassing even the Normandy landings in numbers and logistics. All services played major roles. The navies escorted convoys totalling over 3,000 ships from more than a dozen ports in the Mediterranean, the United Kingdom, and North America, and delivered over 160,000 soldiers to twenty-six beaches between Licata and Siracusa. Airborne assaults led the way in the British and American sectors. Three thousand

Canadian infantrymen train for mountain warfare in the hills of Scotland [e008300270].

aircraft took part in a comprehensive air campaign to destroy enemy airfields and communications.

The most important question that Husky answered for the planners of amphibious operations concerned the related issues of landing zones and supply. Since the two largest ports in Sicily, Palermo and Messina, defied early capture, it would be necessary to supply the armies over the beaches, possibly for up to thirty days, until the ports at Siracusa, Licata, Augusta, and Catania could be put to use. The newly devised amphibious transports, known from their American factory initials as DUKWs, turned out to be (in the estimation of the Royal Army Service Corps) "a magnificent bird … in combined operations the greatest invention of modern times". The DUKW was a six-wheeled truck with a propellor-driven boat built around it. These versatile craft could carry twenty-five men or 3½ tons of equipment at a time, and in the course of a day could ferry 23 tons of equipment from ship to shore. Their performance in Sicily, proving that an invading force could avoid a heavily defended port area and still be assured of a line of supply, was duly noted by the planners of Operation Overlord.

In other respects Husky looks like a rehearsal for Normandy. The cast of characters featured commanders – Eisenhower, Montgomery, Dempsey, Patton, Bradley – whose uneasy working relationships in Sicily portended the sharper clashes to come a year later. In outline, too, Sicily prefigured the Normandy campaign, with slow progress on the British and Canadian fronts, the Americans advancing quickly in a wide sweep, and a hard-won victory diminished by the Allies' failure to trap the retreating German forces. It did not help matters that the commander directing overall operations in Sicily, General Harold Alexander, was not one to lay out precise instructions to his subordinates or to harness them to a carefully defined set of objectives.

All this lay in the future as the planners ironed out the myriad problems inherent in combined operations. One of the last wrinkles involved integrating 1st Canadian Infantry Division and 1st Army Tank Brigade into the Anglo-American order of battle. The Dieppe raid had done nothing to still the voices in Canada clamouring about the inactivity of Canadian troops. Everyone else, even the latecoming Americans, seemed to be doing something. Ever sensitive to public opinion, MacKenzie King pressed the British government in March 1943 to include Canadian units in the forthcoming (but as yet unspecified) operation. Althought this meant dividing the Canadian Army – anathema to General Andrew McNaughton who wished the army to fight as a unified whole, as had the illustrious Canadian Corps in the Great War – the pressure to get Canadians into the fight overrode all other considerations. And so it came to pass that the "Red Patch Division" was added to 30th British Corps

Shermans of 1st Canadian Army Tank Brigade on a tactical exercise in England [e008300271].

Accompanied by Colonel Ian Johnston (left) and Brigadier Howard Graham (middle), Major-General Guy Simonds inspects the 48th Highlanders of Canada [e008300272].

in April 1943 to become part of the illustrious Eighth Army.

Short notice sparked an intensive programme of training and refitting. The three infantry brigades were despatched to Scotland to practise amphibious assaults and mountain warfare; the armoured brigade had to learn the workings of the new Sherman tanks; and the support units, artillerymen, signallers, engineers, service corps, medical teams, and intelligence staffs all had to assemble their wares and go over their routines. In the meantime a tragic accident occasioned the appointment of a new commander. Major-General Harry L.N. Salmon, a well-regarded officer appointed to lead the Canadians in Sicily, died in a plane crash on his way to Cairo for briefings on the forthcoming campaign. Nominated to replace him was Major-General Guy Simonds, whose lack of battle experience was offset by an impressive career and a formidable military intellect.

The 25,000 Canadian soldiers who filed onto the transports in the Clyde estuary in mid June were not yet aware of their destination, but all had the sense that this was the real thing. Shortly after the convoy put to sea, they received notice that they were to take part in a large-scale operation in the Mediterranean. On Dominion Day came confirmation that their target was Sicily. The rest of the voyage was spent getting used to the billowing new khaki uniforms as the rank and file pored over maps, photos, and models to familiarise themselves with their tasks. Mindful of the ancient setting where their war was about to begin, some, like Strome Galloway, saw in their own historic venture shades of the Roman past:

No longer destined to take part in the defence of Britain they were destined to fight in distant climes and over ancient lands. Like the Roman Legionaries of old they had served their time in Britain and were now bound for the Mediterranean; but unlike the Roman Legionaries a voyage to Sicily and Italy did not imply retirement from military service – rather it implied the exact opposite.

Morale was high, but no one entertained illusions that the battle for Sicily would be easy. The landscape alone would test a novice army moving along an inadequate road system or coordinating its operations across the rock-ribbed terrain. Broiling heat would tax the stamina of the Canadians severely in the first few days until they became used to the conditions. They would also have to cope with the delays and extortionate terms of attack that the ground allowed an enemy skilled in defensive warfare to impose. As to the enemy's strength, Allied intelligence had identified two Italian corps, numbering 200,000 men, two German divisions with a total of 32,000 men, and about 30,000 Luftwaffe personnel on the island at the beginning of July. Though numerous, the Italian troops were of doubtful worth. Most were demoralised and longed to see Mussolini's reckless war come to an end. The ill-equipped, poorly trained coastal defence units had done little to fortify the sectors assigned to them. Only one of the four divisions deployed in the interior had seen action. No one could say how hard or how long the Italians would resist once the war came to their shores, but on the other hand no one doubted that the German formations would fight with determination and skill. 15th Panzer Grenadier Division was stationed as a mobile reserve in western Sicily, while the Hermann Goering Panzer Division assumed the same role on the eastern half of the island.

Relations between the Axis partners had deteriorated to the point where the Germans were already planning to take over Italy in the likely event of Mussolini's downfall. During the Sicily campaign control of the battle was to pass from the Italian high command, nominally in charge of all Axis forces on the island, into German hands. As Italian resistance crumbled the Germans added reinforcements to create a separate corps with a strength of 70,000 men. To be noted here are the implications for the embryonic Italian campaign. Although he was resigned to the loss of Sicily, the campaign persuaded Field Marshall Albert Kesselring that strong resistance in southern Italy, where the terrain likewise favoured the defenders, would enable the Germans (with or without the Italians) to wear down Allied strength. His reasoning mirrored the rationale of the British Chiefs of Staff, in that the more resources the Allies committed to the Mediterranean, the fewer they would have for an attack on Germany directly. The seeds of the long attritional struggle to come were sown in Sicily.

William Ogilvie, *Prelude to Invasion* [CWM 19710261-4688].

History

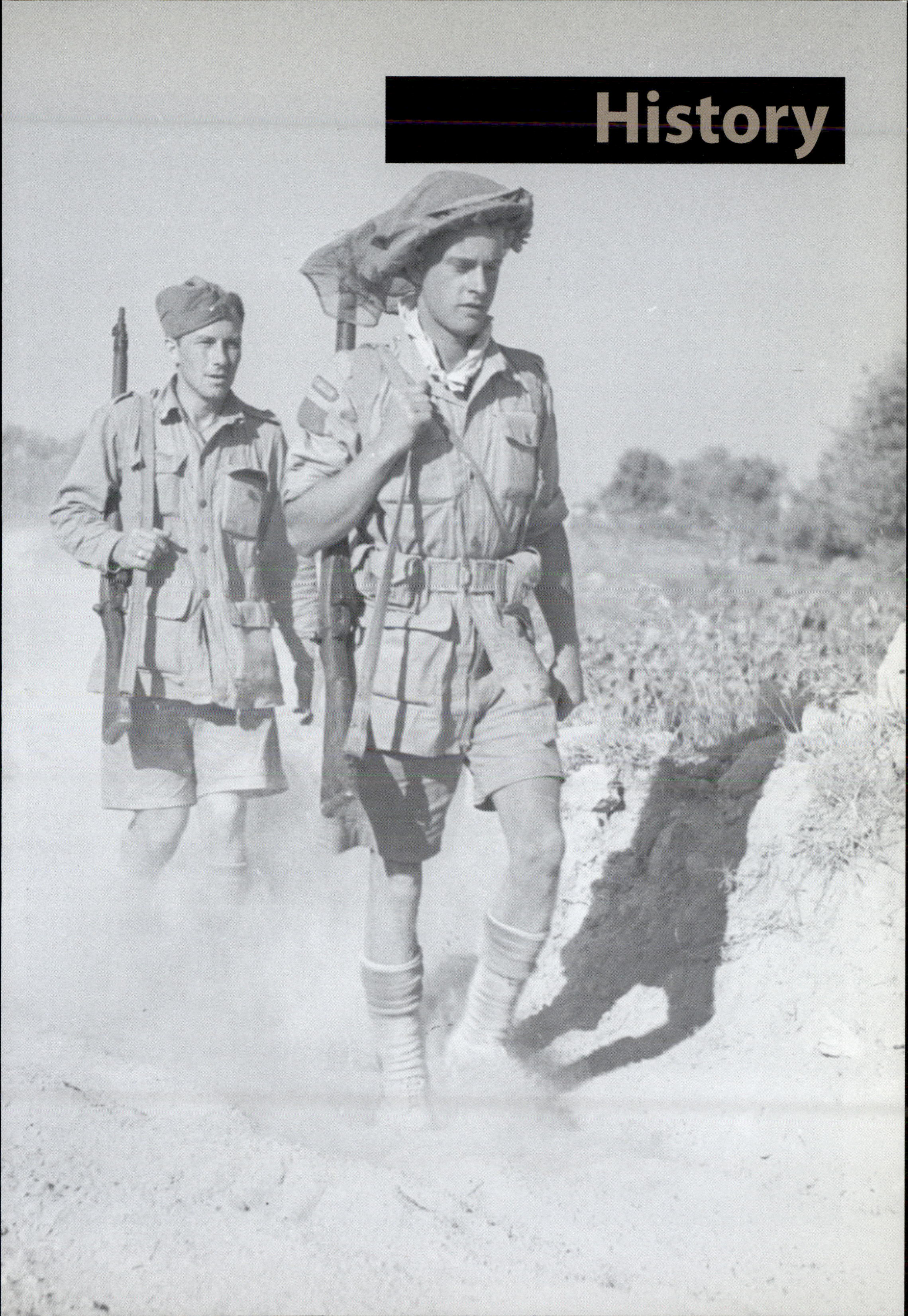

From Pachino to Piazza Armerina:
July 10-17, 1943

Operation Husky called for the Anglo-American forces to land in two main places. U.S. Seventh Army was to come ashore along the southern coast, in the Gulf of Gela, while the British Eighth Army (consisting of 13th and 30th Corps) made its assaults in the Gulf of Noto, along the southeastern corner of Sicily between Pachino and Siracusa. The British sector contained five landing zones, of which two were assigned to 13th Corps. Their landings, near Avola and Cassibile, were preceded by airborne assaults intended to clear the way for the quick capture of Siracusa (Syracuse to English-speakers) and for the subsequent Corps advance to Catania.

The Pachino peninsula on the southeastern tip of Sicily was the area assigned to Lieutenant-General Oliver Leese's 30th Corps. Two British formations, 231st Brigade and 51st (Highland) Division, came in at "Bark East" along the southeastern rim of the peninsula. On the western side, 1st Canadian Division landed at "Bark West", the codename given to the concave shoreline between Punta delle Formiche and Punta Castellazzo. The Canadian zone was subdivided into two sectors, with 1st

Brigade landing on the right at "Roger" and 2nd Brigade on the left at "Sugar". In reserve were 3rd Brigade and the tanks of the Three Rivers Regiment, assigned to follow through at "Sugar" once the Canadians were ashore.

"We skirted the lofty crags and jutting rocks of Pachynus…" – words from Virgil's *Aeneid* echoing the wariness of ancient sailors in rounding the southeastern tip of Sicily would have rung true for the pilots guiding the landing barges to the Pachino beaches in the predawn hours of July 10. After riding out a tremendous gale during the day of July 9, the invasion fleet dropped anchor off the coast of Sicily just after midnight. At 0134 the transports carrying 1st Canadian Division began to release the LCAs (Landing Craft, Assault) and LCTs (Landing Craft, Tank) to the enemy shore under cover of darkness, without the calling card of a preparatory naval barrage. Sandbars just off the Canadian beaches added to the pilots' worries as they steered their vessels across seven miles of choppy seas. The elements favoured 2nd Brigade on its way to "Sugar" beach when the high swell swept the flat-bottomed LCAs over the sandbar. Although

William Ogilvie, *D-Day Tank coming ashore* [CWM 19710261-4496].

the Seaforth Highlanders of Canada were deposited in the wrong place, they and the Princess Patricia's Canadian Light Infantry soon got their bearings and secured their objectives.

The elements were less kind to 1st Brigade. Concerns about the sandbars had led to a change in the assault craft to be used. When the ensuing delay provoked an impatient outburst from the Royal Navy commander ("Will your assault ever start?"), Brigadier Howard Graham sent the Hastings and Prince Edward Regiment and Royal Canadian Regiment off in a mixed flotilla of LCAs and LCTs. As feared, over half of the landing craft grounded on the sandbar. Some then released the smaller DUKWs which relayed the soldiers to the beach, but most of the attackers had to wade 80-100 yards to shore. Despite arriving three hours behind schedule, and in one case five miles from the assigned beach, the assault companies quickly overcame the few Italian defenders willing to put up a fight and secured their objectives at the Pachino airfield and on the Pachino-Ispica road.

Naval gunfire suppressed the last spasms of resistance. By 0645 the Canadian landings were reported successful. Casualties were light, amounting to just seven men killed and twenty-five wounded on the first day. Afterwards,

Bulldozers clear a path for vehicles moving inland [PA 163668].

however, once the full account of the landings was pieced together, all involved counted their blessings. An enemy in well-prepared positions, determined to resist, would have given a rough reception to attackers landing in disarray, one flank open, without tanks, and using weapons clogged by sand or seawater. As the infantrymen moved inland, they looked back at the armada moored offshore and gave thanks for the Allied air supremacy

Men and equipment stream ashore near Pachino during the afternoon of July 10, 1943 [PA 163751].

which permitted such a conglomeration of supply ships and transports to function unmolested by the enemy.

Blackshirt militia made a nuisance of themselves now and then as the Canadians kept pace on the left flank of the Eighth Army. The real adversaries were heat, thirst, and lack of transport. Three supply ships had been sunk en route to Sicily with the loss of 500 vehicles, leaving the infantrymen no alternative but to march through the shadeless, waterless, increasingly hilly terrain in temperatures above 40° C. It became obvious early on that the Italians were "crack troops – they crack every time we hit them", as Farley Mowat waggishly put it, and the narrative of the first three days amounts to little more than a recital of placenames enlivened by the soldiers' reactions to the world around them. Impressions of the land they had come to were vivid ("a Biblical beauty and setting"), if not always favourable. Men who had grown up during the Depression could still be shocked by the poverty.

2nd Brigade made its way through Ispica along Highway 115 to Modica where after a brief skirmish the town fell to the Princess Patricias. Over a thousand Italian soldiers surrendered to an Edmonton Regiment patrol at Scicli while the rest of the battalion and the Seaforths headed for Ragusa. There they met soldiers of the U.S. 45th Division who each, in the eyes of the footsore Canadians, seemed to have his own jeep. Meanwhile 1st Brigade had taken a parallel course to Rosolini before turning north on a secondary road towards Giarratana. "I

William Ogilvie, *Prisoner Type, Pachino, July 1943* [CWM 19710261-4696].

have few coherent memories of that horrendous march … only hazed images obscured as if by the perpetual dust itself," recalled Farley Mowat whose description of the first three days makes palpable the ordeal of the dust-whitened infantrymen, asleep on their feet, tramping dully onwards. Once 1st Brigade reached Giarratana on

An Italian coastal gun near Pachino, abandoned by its crew [e008300273].

July 13 after a 80-kilometre trek, a 36-hour halt allowed the troops to rest while supplies were brought up. It also furnished an occasion for the Eighth Army commander, Lieutenant-General Bernard Montgomery, to give a pep talk to the Canadians in which he warned them of harder fighting to come.

Montgomery's visit coincided with a change of impetus in the Eighth Army's battle. His plan as first conceived had given the leading role to 13th Corps on the British right. Their axis of advance lay along the coast road, Highway 114, running north from Siracusa to the next major objective, Catania, and thence to Messina, whose capture would close the enemy's escape hatch out of Sicily. The Germans were quick to perceive the threat. To avoid the entrapment of the German forces, General Hans Hube was despatched to Sicily four days after the Allied invasion to arrange a phased withdrawal into the northeastern corner of the island opposite the Strait of Messina. The German formations in western Sicily were pulled back to man a series of defensive lines contracting inwards with each stage of the retirement. 15th Panzer Grenadier Division deployed around the road nexus at Enna. The Hermann Goering Panzer Division and two regiments of the hardy 1st Parachute Division took up positions behind the Simeto River to block the British thrust towards Catania. Despite the herculean efforts of the Commandos at Lentini and the Airlanding Brigade at the Primosole Bridge, Montgomery found the 13th Corps' offensive stalled in the Plain of Catania, short of the objectives at Catania and the Gerbini airfields. He therefore shifted the weight of attack to the 30th Corps sector on the left. This change reshaped the campaign and elevated the Canadian part in it.

An overview would be helpful at this point. The battle for Sicily revolved around possession of roads and road junctions, nowhere more so than in the middle of the island. The citadel of Enna governed the road system in all directions, including Highway 117, the main north-south artery through central Sicily. Capturing Enna and gaining control of this road would split the island in half and win access to three east-west roads by which the Allies could turn the German defences in the Plain of Catania. One was Highway 113, running along the northern coast to Messina. Another was Highway 120 which left the 117 at Nicosia and meandered through Troina to Randazzo. The third was Highway 121, leading east from Enna to Adrano (also known as Aderno) on the western slopes of Mount Etna. Montgomery directed 30th Corps to throw a strong left hook at the Germans by driving north and then east along Highways 120 and 121.

Italian equipment left behind on the road near Ispica [e008300275].

The southern slopes of Mount Etna dominate the Catania plain and the eastern shore of Sicily where Montgomery first intended the main British effort to be made.

The springboard was Vizzini, which fell to 51st (Highland) Division late on July 14. From here the 30th Corps advance took the shape of a trident. The 51st pushed northeast through Militello to attack the Gerbini airfields from the flank; 231st (Malta) Brigade set off along a road leading north through Raddusa and across the Dittaino Valley towards Agira; and 1st Canadian Division struck northwest along Highway 124 from Vizzini through Grammichele, Caltagirone, San Michele di Ganzeria to the junction with Highway 117, where they swung north through Piazza Armerina and on towards Enna. The new assignment, however, created a rift between the Allied armies when the Canadians were granted use of Highway 124 ahead of Patton's U.S. 45th Division. The Americans were furious at being shouldered aside when they stood poised to reach Enna days sooner than the Eighth Army could. Even the British Official History concedes that Alexander erred in giving priority to 1st Canadian Division. A prompt advance by the mechanised, comparatively fresh Americans on July 13-14 would have thrown the Germans off balance as they redisposed their forces and would have prevented them from mounting any sustained defence west of Mount Etna.

As it was, the Germans traded space for time as they connected their first defensive line along an arc between Santo Stefano on the northern coast to a point south of Catania on the eastern side. A skirmish on the outskirts of Grammichele temporarily interrupted 1st Brigade's progress on July 15. High ground overlooking the road south of Piazza Armerina enabled German rearguards to hold up the Edmontons when 2nd Brigade led the way

on July 16. By July 17, as 3rd Brigade took the lead towards Enna, the Germans' outer ring of defence was fairly compact. A last British effort to break through in the Plain of Catania only confirmed the stalemate on the right and led Montgomery to modify the Canadians' role. Expecting 1st Canadian Division to reach Enna quickly, he instructed them to thrust along Highway 121 from Leonforte to Adrano, and proposed that the Americans push on to the north coast and then turn east along Highways 113 and 120. To launch their eastward drive as quickly as possible, the Canadians had to get past Valguarnera and across the Dittaino Valley.

Montgomery and Simonds (right) confer, 17 July 1943 [e008300276].

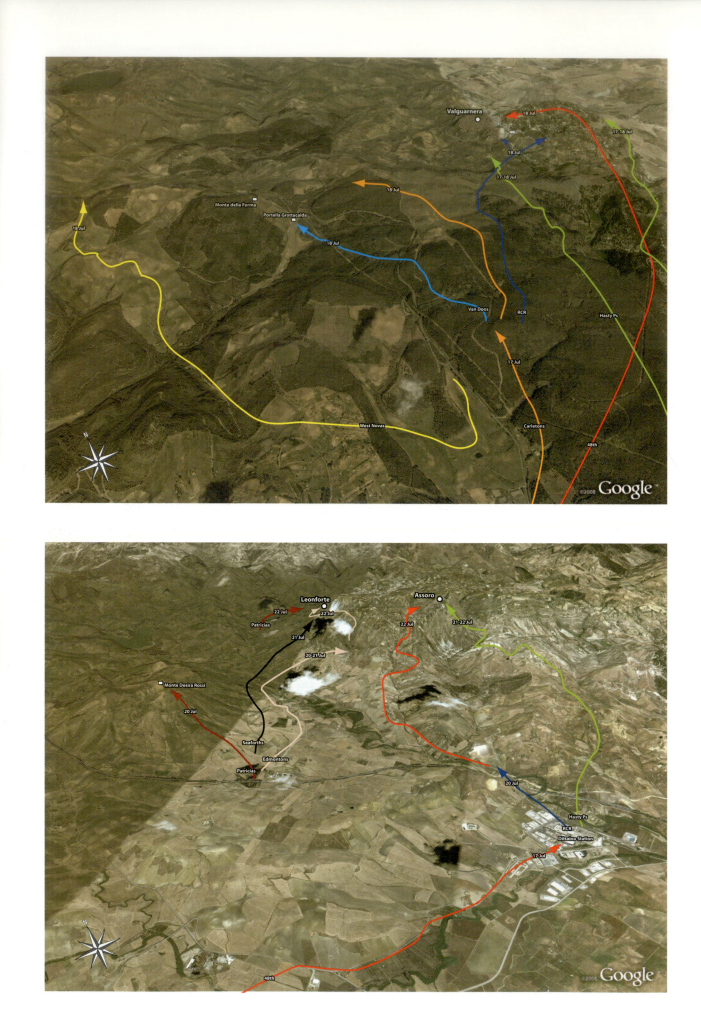

From Valguarnera to Leonforte and Assoro:
July 17-22, 1943

Five miles north of Piazza Armerina, Highway 117 veered northwest to Enna at a place where another road (today the SP 4) ambled east to Valguarnera. This road junction was of obvious tactical importance since it gave access to two routes through the Dittaino Valley. It also made a natural defensive site since Highway 117 ran through a narrow corridor (known as the Portella Grottacalda) on the way to the junction. The highest of the surrounding hills, Monte della Forma, dominated the junction and gave the Germans a grandstand view over the Canadians' advance.

The handiwork of German demolition teams slowed passage along the highway and forced the infantry of 3rd Brigade out of their carriers as they approached the Portella Grottacalda. Patrols detected the presence of the enemy around the road junction. Late in the day of July 17, after the leading tanks and infantry had subdued the German outposts in front of the Portella Grottacalda,

Simonds ordered the brigade to push through to the road junction. That evening the Van Doos attacked through the Portella Grottacalda and spent fourteen hours under fire as they duelled with the Panzer Grenadiers perched in the heights on either side. Early on July 18 the Carletons commenced a right-flanking attack towards the feature on the northeast edge of the junction that forced the Germans to retire from their positions on Monte della Forma. This action complemented a sweep to the left by the West Nova Scotias who withdrew behind a hill south of Monte della Forma. Using the feature as a screen, they moved across country to seize high ground dominating the Enna road about a mile west of Monte della Forma. The three-pronged assault gained the road junction by late afternoon on July 18.

Valguarnera fell to the 48th Highlanders during the night of July 18-19 after twenty-four hours of hard fighting by 1st Brigade. The previous night, the Hasty Ps set off on

William Ogilvie, *Self-propelled artillery engaging enemy positions* [CWM 19710261-4740].

West Novas in slit trenches near Valguarnera [e008300277].

withdrawing in the face of an enemy counterattack. A mile and a half to the right, 'A' and 'C' companies reached a knoll overlooking an east-west lateral road that served as a line of communications across the German front. 'A' company shot up half a dozen truckloads of infantry that came rolling into their gunsights, but intense mortar fire and the arrival of enemy reinforcements forced both companies to retire. Both actions inflicted heavy losses on the Germans and distracted them from the main task of defending the road junction. The RCRs also closed in on Valguarnera during the morning of July 18, fighting their way to within half a mile of the town before being held off by three tanks guarding the entrance. Sent in to complete the capture, the 48th moved up on the right flank and eliminated a series of machine gun posts barring the way. Patrols slipped into the town and reported it clear of the enemy.

a ten-mile trek through the darkness and broken country, press-ganging a farmer into service as a guide. By dawn the wandering companies found themselves ensconced in the hills on either side of the town. On the left, 'B' and 'D' companies cut the road where it turned north into Valguarnera and knocked out a convoy of vehicles before

Valguarnera was a sign of things to come. The two-day battle cost 145 casualties, including forty men killed, and exposed the difficulties that the Canadians would meet repeatedly over the next two weeks. Command and control proved hard to exercise at any level when communications were prone to break down. In one

William Ogilvie, *Approach to Assoro* [CWM 19710261-4413].

instance the RCRs' padre had to carry a message back on foot to put the battalion commander in the picture. Contact and cohesion between platoons manoeuvring through the crumpled terrain were also highly frangible. Even if the riflemen reached their objectives, mortar teams, ammunition bearers, and supporting arms found it difficult to keep up, leaving the forward companies without the means to deal with enemy fire or counterattacks. The initiative and skill of small pockets of men became the deciding factor. It is significant that half the medals awarded after the Valguarnera action went to enterprising sergeants, corporals, and privates who carried out the small but vital actions that tipped the scales in favour of the Canadian attackers.

Having lost a day, Simonds left Enna to the Americans while he spurred his brigades on to their objectives on the far side of the Dittaino Valley. Standing as gateposts at the western end of the massif facing the Canadians were the towns of Leonforte and Assoro. Both were ancient settlements built with defence in mind. Shielded by cliffs and ravines, each afforded but one entrance, and their defenders could see for miles from the neighbouring heights. Neither surprise nor direct assault seemed practicable options, but the towns had to be taken if the Canadians were to thrust east along Highway 121.

Some of the most beautiful landscape in Sicily greeted the eyes of the Seaforths who led the 2nd Brigade advance towards Leonforte early on July 19. Three miles beyond Valguarnera harassing fire drove them to ground until mortars and artillery could be brought up to make reply. The Patricias then passed through to high ground astride the road to Leonforte, allowing the Edmontons to stake out a position within striking distance of the town on July 20. A German detachment on Monte Desira Rossi remained a thorn in the Edmontons' side which the Patricias excised that evening.

While 2nd Brigade prepared to tackle Leonforte, 1st Brigade was testing the approaches to Monte Assoro. Named after a king Assorus of the Sicels (the ancient people who gave their name to the island), the peak presented a daunting spectacle from the brigade's base at the Dittaino Station, soaring more than 3,000 feet over the valley floor and 1,000 feet over the base of the cliff on the eastern side. It was capped by the ruins of a castle that had evolved from a Byzantine stronghold to an Arab fortress to a Norman enceinte built during the reign of Roger II, whose forebear Robert Guiscard had begun "the other Norman conquest" in a campaign through the Dittaino Valley in 1061. Nine centuries on, young men from Canada were to add their own feats of arms to the historical record.

A single road wound like a corkscrew up the escarpment to meet the main street into Assoro on the western edge of the town. Brigadier Graham and his battalion commanders saw it as the road to perdition and sought an alternative route,

In this 1944 photo, a Sicilian peasant leads a mule train near the southern approaches to Assoro; the photographer notes that the Hasty Ps scaled the eastern (i.e. right-hand) slope [e008300289].

Assoro from the south. The winding road was the route taken by the 48th Highlanders in their assault on the town.

but when the Hasty Ps' commander, Lieutenant-Colonel Bruce Sutcliffe, and his intelligence officer, Captain Battle Cockin, went forward to reconnoitre, an .88 shell killed the former and mortally wounded the latter. Cockin clung to life long enough to warn the succeeding commander, Major Lord John Tweedsmuir, "John, for God's sake, don't go up that road." As Farley Mowat recalled, Tweedsmuir, son of a Governor-General of Canada, English peer, soldier and adventurer,

looked up at the towering colossus of Assoro with the visionary eye of a Lawrence of Arabia, and saw that the only way to accomplish the impossible was to attempt the impossible. He thereupon decided that the battalion would make a right-flank march by night across the intervening trackless gullies to the foot of the great cliff, scale that precipitous wall and, just at dawn, take the summit by surprise.

This they did, in an exploit now legendary. After Bren carriers transported the five hundred riflemen as far forward as possible, a select assault force led "a sinuous human centipede crawling on hundreds of awkward feet

into the gathering darkness." With less than an hour to spare, their hearts sank when they came to a ravine at the foot of the cliff, and again during the climb when one false crest gave way to another as they neared the summit. Day was breaking as the first parties reached the top. So certain were the Germans that the eastern side

The chasm guarding the southern tip of Leonforte [PA 188917].

A soldier of the Canadian Provost Corps stands near a destroyed German vehicle in Leonforte [PA 205234].

was insurmountable that the Hasty Ps achieved complete surprise. They quickly overwhelmed an artillery spotting team and took possession of the three-acre summit.

The German response was not long in coming. Throughout the sweltering day of July 21 the Hasty Ps endured mortar fire and shelling from the enemy batteries on the massif east of Leonforte, and then stood off an attack from the town below late that evening. Years later, Tweedsmuir attributed the battalion's success in holding its rocky perch to a mule and three miracles. The first was a powerful wireless set, borne by the worthy beast of burden to the base of the cliff and by men to the top, which ensured communications; the second was the capture of a state of the art German range finder which the Canadians used to pinpoint the location of the German guns; and the third was Major Bert Kennedy's ability to dredge up from memory's recesses the artillery training received years before to direct Canadian fire upon German gun positions, supply lines, and counterattacks. A relief party, made up of 100 volunteers from 'D' company of the Royal Canadian Regiment, slipped "under the very noses of the Germans" to bring much needed rations and ammunition to the isolated Hasty Ps during the night of July 21-22.

The 48th Highlanders completed the capture of Assoro with an epic climb of their own on the night of July 21-22. The men of 'B' company used each other as human ladders to scale the forty-foot terrace steps along the left hand side of the road up to the town, while 'D' company performed similar acrobatics on the right. During the morning of July 22 the two companies huddled beneath the crest to allow a mortar and artillery barrage to pummel the defences and then overran the defenders on the heights southwest of the town. By mid-morning

Sergeant Russell McPhee, one of the Royal Canadian Engineers who assembled the vital replacement bridge near Leonforte, speaks with Montgomery and Simonds in August, 1943 [e008300285].

they had a stranglehold over the T-junction on the western edge of Assoro. When fighting patrols entered the town the Germans quickly decamped to avoid being trapped between the Hasty Ps above and the 48th below. Tanks and support vehicles could now move up the road to consolidate the Canadian position at Assoro.

The 2nd Brigade attack on Leonforte began inauspiciously when a salvo of Canadian shells struck an 'Orders' Group convened on a knoll southeast of the town. Before dawn on July 21 two Seaforth platoons had already tried to break into the southern end of Leonforte by crossing the deep ravine that separated the brigade from its objective, but they were left stranded on the outskirts once daylight exposed them to German fire from the heights above. Brigadier Chris Vokes ordered the Seaforths to take the town behind a massive barrage, only to reassign the task to the Edmontons when the officers preparing the attack were killed or wounded by their own artillery. Supported by heavy machine gun fire from the Saskatoon Light Infantry, the Edmontons clambered across the ravine after sunset and followed a curtain of shells into the town. 'A' and 'D' companies got well into Leonforte on both sides of the main street before the Germans reacted with tanks and infantry. Through the night of July 21-22 'B' and 'C' companies joined the confused house-to-house fighting that swept up and down the length of the town. When wireless commmunications failed, Lieutenant-Colonel Jim Jefferson entrusted a note to a Sicilian boy ("To any British or Canadian officer") who fell in with a patrol on his way to the Canadian lines and passed on the message that the Edmontons badly needed help. Relieved that the Edmontons were still of this world, Vokes put together a mixed battle group of Patricias, Three Rivers Regiment tanks, and anti-tank guns to rush to their aid.

The road into Leonforte bent in a hairpin turn at a bridge over the ravine. The bridge had been blown up by the Germans, so as the fighting raged in the town, sappers of the 3rd Field Company toiled in the darkness, under fire, to build a crossing. By 0900 on July 22 the replacement bridge was ready. The flying column hurtled down the road, over the bridge, and back up the switchback into

William Ogilvie, *Street scene, Assoro, Sicily* [CWM 19710261-4779].

Leonforte. Near the town centre a German tank emerged on to main street and was destroyed at ten yards range by a Three Rivers Sherman that was faster on the draw. Bands of Seaforths joined with the Edmontons and Patricias to clear the town from south to north. Two companies of Patricias then grappled with German detachments on the heights on either side of the town's northern edge. In the course of these actions Private Sidney Cousins destroyed two enemy machine gun nests in a singlehanded charge over 150 yards of open ground. His heroism would surely have supplemented the total of 21 medals given to Canadian soldiers for bravery at Leonforte had he not been killed by a stray shell later that day. In this case the regulations concerning military awards restricted recognition to Mentioned in Dispatches.

The same day that the Canadians secured Assoro and Leonforte, the Americans entered Palermo. The next day, U.S. 1st Division reached Highway 120 at Petralia, and U.S. 45th Division Highway 113 west of Cefalu. Both could now turn east in concert with the Canadian drive along Highway 121. While 1st and 2nd Brigades prepared to take Agira, 3rd Brigade deployed for a parallel advance through the Dittaino Valley towards Catenanuova. To assist the Canadian operations, the Devons, Dorsets, and

This Canadian Battlefields Foundation plaque was placed on the summit of Assoro in 2004 to commemorate the achievements of the Hastings and Prince Edward Regiment.

Hampshires of the British 231st Brigade came under Simonds's command. Known as the "Malta Brigade" from their service on that redoubtable island bastion, the British formations would strike north from Raddusa towards points east of Agira to cut off the German line of retreat. The Anglo-American forces seemed poised to deliver the coup de grace, but to the Canadians it was evident from Leonforte and Assoro that the Germans meant business "now that we are nearing something like a serious defence zone."

The view from Assoro towards Agira, the Canadian objective after the capture of Assoro and Leonforte [Matt Symes].

Sicily History

The advance to Agira:
July 23-28, 1943

Even before the fighting died down during the afternoon of July 22, Simonds was issuing orders for the capture of Agira. This next objective lay eight miles from Leonforte across the rugged plateau bisected by Highway 121. A little to the east of Leonforte was an important junction with Highway 117, and two miles further on the village of Nissoria was nestled in a hollow between two ridge lines. To establish a firm base, the 48th Highlanders were to secure the junction, enabling the RCRs to move down the 121 to Nissoria. There the two following companies would pass through to carry the RCR advance to the fringes of Agira, which would then be stormed. The Hasty Ps and 48th Highlanders would trail closely behind in order to exploit beyond Agira.

"It was time to get out the whips and to spare neither men nor machines," wrote the Division's diarist concerning an attack that was to be the work of a day. The timetable and the reliance on a single battalion advance reflect Simonds's assumption that the German opposition would be concentrated around Agira, when in fact the ground east of Nissoria gave the defenders concealment, good lines of fire, and reverse slopes offering shelter from artillery shells. In this terrain the Germans were adept at shifting their placement and weapons to confuse assessments of their strength and dispositions.

Things got off to a rough start when the 48th ran into an ambush at the highway junction on the night of July 22-23. By morning the Germans had gone, and the RCRs moved up to the base for their assault. After a day's delay to conduct reconnaissance, the set-piece attack began at 1400 on July 24 "with a timed artillery programme, report lines, bells, train whistles, and all the trimmings," under the gaze of the Canadian commanders watching from the crest of Assoro. The gunners would cloak the advance with smoke shells 1,000 yards in advance of the infantry, who would also be accompanied by tanks of The Three Rivers

Canadian officers monitor the assaults on Agira in William Ogilvie's *Command Post, Assoro* [CWM 19710261-4476].

The scars of battle in Nissoria. The road running through the town is Highway 121 [e008300278].

who knocked out ten Shermans, although the Three Rivers tank crews replied with a number of hits on German tanks and anti-tank guns. The air support from the medium bombers failed to materialise.

Colonel Ralph Crowe of the RCRs, up with the forward units, tried to keep the attack going. He despatched 'D' company to capture the high ground on the left of the road, where a red Casa Cantoniera made a prominent landmark, but they could make no headway. Neither could 'A' and 'B' companies on the right until they began to work their way around the flank where they happened upon a long defile that led almost all the way to Agira. The two companies sent word back to 'C' company which followed them around the southern edge of the ridge. In so doing, however, they departed from the plan, and no one could figure out where they were. Colonel Crowe was killed when he went forward to ascertain their whereabouts; his successor could locate only the survivors of 'D' company around Nissoria. Out of touch, in tactical limbo, the three companies spent the better part of July 24-25 well behind the enemy positions.

Regiment and assisted by dive-bombers of the Desert Air Force. 'C' and 'D' companies quickly cleared Nissoria, but when 'A' and 'D' companies passed through to the ridge line a mile beyond the town they came under heavy mortar and machine-gun fire. At this critical moment, the wireless sets gave out, reducing communications to relays of runners between the companies. The barrage soon outdistanced the infantrymen and the covering smoke was dispersed by the wind. The tanks, unable to move off-road, made easy prey for the German anti-tank gunners

The flash from a Canadian 25-pounder lights up the night near Nissoria, 27 July 1943 [DND ZK-860-6].

William Ogilvie, *Night Shoot* [CWM 19710261-4653].

The ridgeline codenamed "LION", immediately east of Nissoria, formed the first objective in the Canadian push to Agira. The Casa Cantoniera nicknamed "The Red Schoolhouse" stands beside the yellow building on the far right.

Inexplicably, when their location was confirmed during the morning of July 25, the companies were called back, even though the Germans seemed oblivious to the open door on their left. As historian Bill McAndrew has commented, "if they could be extricated, they could also have been reinforced. Why a battalion – or a brigade – was not sent round remains a mystery."

Trying to focus the blurred tactical picture in front of him, Simonds kept to his plan and sent the Hasty Ps against the German blocking positions that night. No tanks, no artillery, no reconnaissance – Major Tweedsmuir had time only to outline an impromptu plan of attack. He had his companies advance steathily towards the ridge on the south side of the road. They nearly achieved surprise but were detected among the German outposts. For nearly two hours the riflemen returned fire against the panoply of machine guns, mortars, and dug-in tanks arrayed against them. Dispersed and low on ammunition, their commander wounded, the companies withdrew at daylight. Eighty casualties made it the Hasty Ps' worst single day in Sicily.

To keep up the pressure, Simonds ordered one more piecemeal attack in the evening of July 25. This time the 48th Highlanders attempted to carry the high ground north of the highway. 'B' company was to reach the summit of Monte di Nissoria on the far left, paving the way for 'D' company to attack a lower eminence to the right, and then for 'C' company to take the height where the Casa Cantoniera – now known to the Canadians as "the Red

Schoolhouse" – stood beside the highway. Following a short barrage 'B' company dodged fire from a knoll to their left and soon reported themselves on the objective. Their success was illusory, however, since they had gained only a false crest below the summit. A desperate attempt to rush the German positions on top was turned back. 'D' company found itself pinned down. Neither company could establish wireless contact to advise battalion HQ of their predicament or coordinate artillery fire, and both had to withdraw. On the right, 'C' company nearly salvaged the operation when it got close enough to send patrols to the area around the Red Schoolhouse. When they reported the area clear, 'C' company prepared to seize the place, only to be called back. In his account of the action Colonel Ian Johnston stated that the company had been withdrawn in the face of solid enemy defence, but this is contradicted by the regimental history which airs the company's frustrations at being recalled just when the objective seemed within their grasp.

Coming so soon after its accomplishments at Leonforte and Assoro, 1st Brigade's repulse at Nissoria bit deeply, all the more so when the commanders cast blame on the infantry for failing to stay close behind the barrage. As the RCR historian tersely retorts, "what [the commanders] had planned was not a battle but a walkover." "You can't follow fire support closely when climbing a cliff," was the 48th Highlanders' rebuttal. In retrospect, expectations exceeded realities. The expanse of ground was too vast for the shell-rationed artillery to cover, the distance and terrain too imposing for the infantry to keep pace, especially when communications failed and the enemy did not react as expected.

These factors were taken into account when 2nd Brigade resumed the attack on the evening of July 26. The new plan set three intermediate objectives: the ridgeline east of Nissoria was designated "LION"; a second, higher ridgeline a mile further on was "TIGER"; and a final barrier on the western approach to Agira became "GRIZZLY". Instead of a single-battalion thrust to Agira, two battalions would advance stage by stage. The Princess Patricias would send 'C' and 'D' companies from a start line west of Nissoria to take "LION." Then 'A' and 'B' would follow through to "TIGER," at which point the Seaforth Highlanders would push through to "GRIZZLY." Three Canadian and two British artillery regiments would carry out a comprehensive fire plan, saturating the first enemy position with an intense concentration and then leading the infantry to the next objective with a creeping barrage lifting every three minutes.

The opening phase of the attack went like clockwork. The Germans holding "LION" were obliterated by the avalanche of shells that descended upon them, and their defences were quickly overrun by the Patricias who arrived two minutes after the bombardment lifted. In the darkness and confusion the next wave of Patricias lost their

way, but Colonel Bert Hoffmeister had kept his Seaforths on the heels of the attack. When at midnight Brigadier Vokes decided to commit the Seaforths, Hoffmeister sent two companies ahead. As much by accident as by design, Major Bell-Irving guided 'A' company onto the objective at "TIGER" on the northern side of the road. 'C' company fought its way over the second ridge early the next morning thanks to timely support from tanks and artillery. Now the tables were turned as the Canadians profited from the high ground to bring fire down on the Germans retreating across the plateau or through the adjacent Salso valley.

While bombers and artillery softened the approaches to Agira, the Seaforths prepared to assault the last features before the town. "GRIZZLY" consisted of two natural battlements. Guarding the southwestern corner was the flat-topped Monte Fronte. On the northwestern corner, the walled communal cemetery on a hill overlooking the junction of the 121 with the road from Troina made a solid defensive bastion; beside it was the lofty dome of Monte Crapuzza. The Seaforths attacked with three companies in the afternoon of July 27. 'D' company met stern resistance at Cemetery Hill and had to pause to restore communications and await reinforcements. 'C' company swung out to the right to take Monte Fronte from the flank but strayed onto two hills south of the objective. 'A' company's exploits, however, rival those of the 1st Brigade at Assoro. When the leading platoon came under fire, the riflemen responded in textbook fashion

In this photo Agira is under bombardment from the Desert Air Force. Note the features marking "GRIZZLY" – the anvil-shaped Monte Fronte to the right, and the dome of Monte Crapuzza visible through the smoke to the left [e008300279].

Monte Fronte from the south. The Seaforths scaled the heights at this end and then swept the defenders from the flat summit.

with fire and movement to gain the base of the hill, while Major Bell-Irving led the other platoons around to the steep southern slope. Here they climbed up to the top and caught the German defenders by surprise. They clung to their foothold through the night, inspired by Lieutenant Harling who "stood up his full height and threw grenades at the oncoming enemy – one after another – singing a Hawaiian song at the top of his lungs." The next morning they cleared the feature with the assistance of 'C' company,

To the north, the Edmontons had been called in to capture the troublesome Cemetery Hill. Previously, an Edmonton detachment had gone across country to cut the Troina-Agira road and play havoc with the German road traffic. Now the battalion made a wide swing to the left to close in on Monte Crapuzza and the cemetery. 'A' company found Monte Crapuzza unoccupied, whereas 'B' company became locked in a fierce fight on the northern side of the cemetery. A section of 'D' company then worked around to the right. Its forty men helped to rout 150 defenders, freeing the way into Agira. A final bombardment and assault were called off when the

Patricias met only pockets of resistance in the town. After a few hours of mopping up, Agira was in Canadian hands by evening on July 28.

A patrol from the Princess Patricias make its way along the main street into Agira, 28 July 1943 [PA 138269].

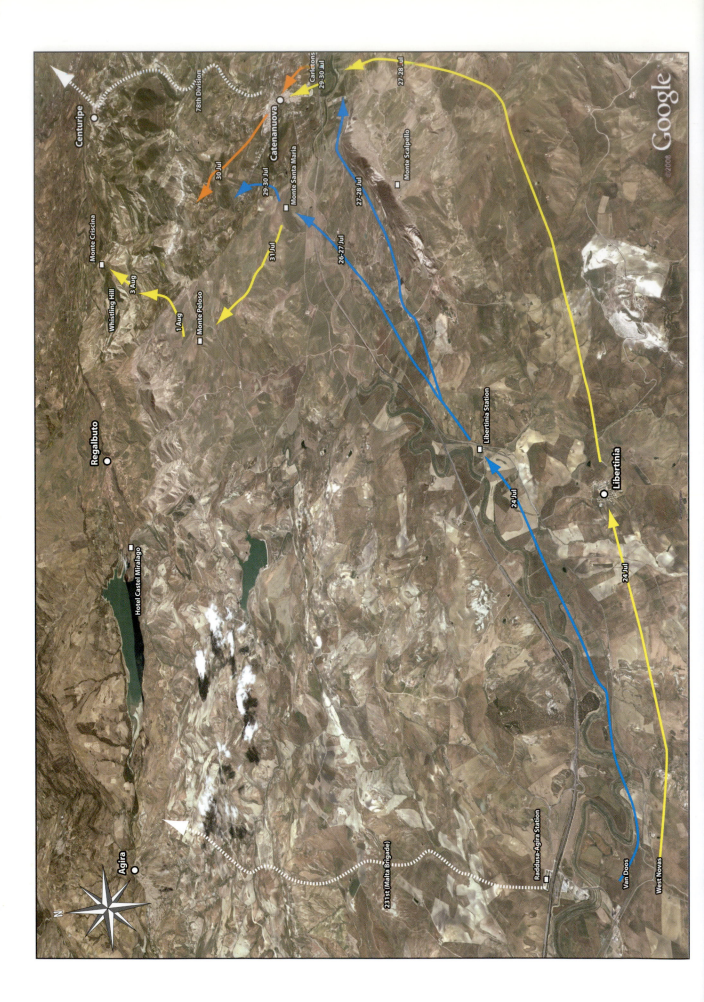

3rd Brigade in the Dittaino Valley:
July 24-August 3, 1943

The part played by 3rd Brigade is somewhat neglected in accounts of the Sicily campaign. Where the terrain and tactical challenges dramatise the 1st and 2nd Brigades' battles at Leonforte, Assoro and Agira, 3rd Brigade's operations in the Dittaino Valley seem workmanlike in comparison. The brigade's actions were not well documented at the time and the regimental histories are vague on many points. The brigade also spent much of the campaign under British command, in an ancillary role, but this should not obscure the exploits of each regiment in the hard fighting around Catenanuova and in the mountainous terrain to the north.

During the week of heavy fighting along the road to Agira, 3rd Brigade was advancing on a parallel course along Highway 192, through the Dittaino valley towards Catenanuova. As drab a place today as it was in 1943, Catenanuova was nonetheless an important objective since it stood on two key roads. One led north to Regalbuto, slated for capture once Agira had been taken, and the other rose with the terrain northeast to Centuripe, a village lodged high over Highway 121 and the Salso River valley.

A week of patrolling east of the Agira-Raddusa rail station brought the brigade to the hamlet of Libertinia and the railway stop of the same name by July 26. That day Brigadier Penhale received orders to capture Catenanuova as quickly as possible, but in order to do so, two features commanding the route to the town would have to be wrested from the enemy. The lesser of the two was Monte Santa Maria, an 800-foot mound on the north bank of the Dittaino. On the southern side of the river, Monte Scalpello formed a long, rocky wall standing 3,000 feet over the western approaches to Catenanuova.

The task of seizing these preliminary objectives was allotted to the Van Doos and West Novas. Starting from Libertinia Station, 'A' company of the Van Doos would strike across the river to take Monte Santa Maria, while 'B' company would clear the northern slope of Monte Scalpello. The West Novas would set out from Libertinia to swing around the other side of Monte Scalpello and face up to Catenanuova from the south.

During the night of July 26-27, the Van Doos' 'A' company filtered along the dry riverbed using a route tested the previous evening. They paused to allow Captain

Tanks of The Three Rivers Regiment raise clouds of dust as they move through the Dittaino Valley [e008300284].

The long hog's back of Monte Scalpello flanks the route taken by 3rd Brigade in its advance along the SS 192 towards its objective at Catenanuova.

Leo Bouchard to call down a quick bombardment, and then crossed a ploughed field to the foot of the hill. The platoons fanned out to tackle the enemy machine gun nests on the slope and fought their way to the top in a bayonet charge. In this attack Lieutenant Guy Robitaille won a Military Cross for exercising skilful leadership despite receiving three serious wounds. The Van Doos stood fast under enemy fire during the day of July 27, repelling several counterattacks, but were forced to vacate Monte Santa Maria under cover of darkness when neither reinforcements nor artillery support could be made available.

Meanwhile, 'B' company came upon a helpful French-speaking "Italienne" who provided information about the paths along the northern slope of Monte Scalpello and the location of the enemy. Like their comrades on Monte Santa Maria, the soldiers of 'B' company were left to their own devices when the time came to deal with the enemy at the eastern tip of the mountain. A quick charge supported only by a few mortars drove off the enemy who retired from his positions south of the Dittaino. This success, however, left the French Canadians exposed to enemy fire after 'B' and 'C' companies occupied the bare ground east of Monte Scalpello. The regimental historian comments on the German tactic of leaving paths open to the infantry while sowing the terrain with mines to delay the passage of vehicles and support weapons, which left the forward companies isolated and unsupplied. The Van Doos found themselves in this very predicament during July 27-28 until the sappers could finally clear the way for vehicles. Once the West Novas had completed their trek around the southern side of Monte Scalpello, 3rd Brigade stood poised to complete the capture of Catenanuova; but at this point, preparations for a renewed effort by 30th Corps towards Adrano imposed a day's delay.

Montgomery had brought the 78th Division to Sicily to lend its weight to 30th Corps. 3rd Brigade now came under British command to assist the newly arrived formation in Operation "Hardgate." The plan called for 78th and 51st Divisions to break the German defensive line on the west side of Mount Etna by capturing Adrano and Paterno respectively, which would in turn compel the Germans to give up their defences in the Plain of Catania. Simultaneously, the Americans would keep pressing towards Messina and Randazzo in "a sustained and relentless drive until the enemy is decisively defeated". The capture of Catenanuova by 3rd Brigade, scheduled for the night of July 29-30, would provide 78th Division with the base for its thrust through Centuripe to Adrano.

Lieutenant-Colonel Paul Bernatchez insisted that his Van Doos be given the task of retaking Monte Santa Maria as the 3rd Brigade assault was being planned. The Van Doos would then capture Hill 204 a thousand yards beyond. The West Novas would break into Catenanuova from their positions across the river, and then seize the high ground overlooking the town from the north. They would be augmented by a company from the Carleton and Yorks that would assist in the capture of the town and then send patrols up the two roads.

The West Novas surged into Catenanuova behind a heavy barrage that seemed to take the fight out of the defenders. The Royal Artillery greatly eased the Van Doos' task in repossessing Monte Santa Maria, but 'D' company found the way to Hill 204 hotly contested. A narrow, dry streambed wound north from the river past the eastern side of Monte Santa Maria and on towards the objective. Lieutenant André Langlais led his platoons along this covered approach for a thousand yards until they came to a small viaduct that resembled a stone house. Around this position the Germans had deployed machine guns and an .88 gun which Langlais methodically directed his platoons to knock out. By 1015 'D' company reported their objective taken.

In the hills ringing the northern edge of Catenanuova the Germans put up a stiffer fight than they had in the

town. German artillery ranged on the Dittaino crossings severed the line of supply and prevented reinforcements from reaching the forward companies. While tanks and SP guns came down the Centuripe road, small bands of German infantry worked through the folds in the terrain to assault the West Novas dug into the shallow scrapes the hard ground yielded. "In as sharp and successful an action as any fought by a Canadian battalion in Sicily" the enemy counterattacks were beaten off, thanks to the stubborn defenders and to presence of mind shown by Lieutenant Ross Guy. After taking a crash course in artillery spotting over the wireless, he used his newfound expertise to call fire down on the enemy infantry swarming around the fringes of his own position.

For the next week, 3rd Brigade worked alongside British units to guard 78th Division's left flank as it made the difficult ascent towards Centuripe. The brigade's main tasks consisted of securing tactically important high points. Monte Peloso was taken without a fight by the West Novas on July 31, but the subsequent bound towards Monte Criscina proved costly and frustrating to the Maritime regiments. The Carletons fought a confused action at Hill 500, east of the Catenanuova-Regalbuto road, as part of a foray into the hills south of Monte Criscina. On their left, the West Novas set off across a ridge line dubbed "Whistling Hill" in an attempt to secure the lofty Monte Criscina, which they believed to be unoccupied. A well-equipped detachment of German paratroopers was in fact solidly emplaced on the feature. The absence of artillery support and the commanding position of the enemy created a mismatch between attackers and defenders, with results evident in the Agira war cemetery where nineteen West Nova Scotia headstones bear the date 2 August 1943.

The sprawling mound of Monte Santa Maria, captured twice by the Royal 22e Régiment, commands the approaches to Catenanuova from the south and southwest.

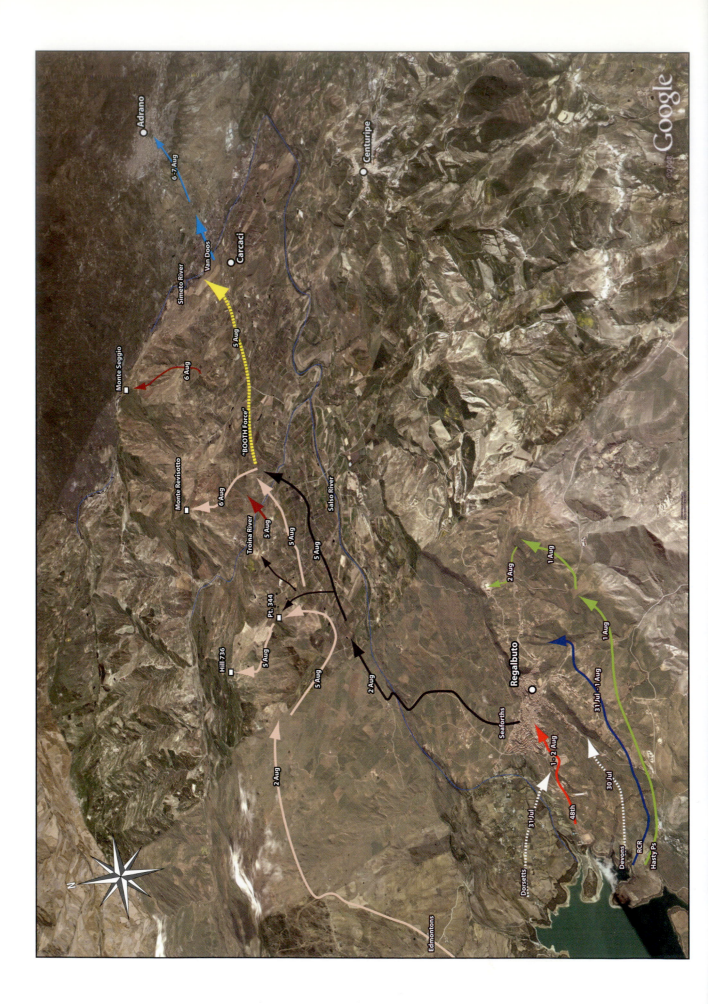

From Regalbuto to Adrano:
July 29 - August 6, 1943

The weary battalions resting after the capture of Agira were soon on their way east again as vital cogs in Operation Hardgate. As 3rd Brigade cleared the way for the 78th Division's attack towards Centuripe, 1st and 2nd Brigades, together with the British 231st Brigade, were to secure the 78th's left flank by capturing Regalbuto and clearing the Salso River valley as far as the Simeto River. Completion of these tasks would give free rein to the 78th Division in its subsequent thrust along Highway 121 to Adrano.

For their part, the Germans intended to mount a determined defence in Regalbuto. They regarded this town and Centuripe as natural strongholds protecting Adrano, the key to their defences in the so-called Etna Line. At Regalbuto the British and Canadians would face the Engineer Battalion of the Hermann Goering Division (old foes from Grammichele) which had strict orders to stand firm. Their readiness to obey orders became clear when the Hampshires came under heavy fire near Regalbuto on the night of July 29. From the long rampart of the Regalbuto ridge, and from the round top of Monte Serione, German machine guns, mortars, and anti-tank guns enfiladed the approaches to the town from the west. Over the next two days, the Devons and Dorsets displayed their battleworthiness in taking the two heights – the

Devons receiving warm praise from the Canadians for their stouthearted performance in holding the Regalbuto ridge against frenzied counterattacks by the Hermann Goerings.

It was left to 1st Brigade to complete the capture of Regalbuto. The 48th Highlanders relieved the Dorsets at Monte Serione and spent the first two days of August sparring with the Germans on the northwestern corner of the town. 'C' company came face to face with enemy tanks as it worked forward from the communal cemetery into the outskirts, and nervously contemplated its chances of holding on without supplies or supporting arms, but the Germans did not attack. 'A' and 'B' companies put platoons in and around the walls of the cemetery to gain shelter from tank and mortar fire. When a stream of Devonshire infantry withdrew from the town down the road in front of the cemetery the 48th were well situated to pour fire into their pursuers.

The RCRs made the first attempt to secure the town. In the predawn hours of August 1, three companies slipped around the southern side of the Regalbuto ridge and headed for the objective on Tower Hill. What had not been sufficiently appreciated was a deep cleft, known as the Cerementario ravine, that split the town on its southern side. The RCRs had little choice but to send one company

Regalbuto from the perspective of the Devons and Dorsets who led the attack on July 30-31, 1943. To the left, Monte Serione and the communal cemetery. To the right, the Regalbuto Ridge and the Tower Hill feature just beyond.

The two hills south of Regalbuto captured by the Hasty Ps. In the foreground, Monte Tiglio; beyond, Monte San Giorgio.

at a time, in pitch black, down the 80-100 foot slope and up the other side. Once the riflemen had clambered up to the far lip, they found resistance too strong to overcome without artillery and support weapons. A platoon sent up to Tower Hill was cut off and one section forced to surrender. The companies stranded at the gorge endured a long, frustrating day under the Sicilian sun and enemy fire until nightfall when they could finally extricate themselves.

Recognising the enemy's determination to hold on, Simonds eschewed a frontal assault and sought instead to envelop the town. He had already directed 2nd Brigade to send patrols well to the northeast of Regalbuto in preparation for an advance through the Salso valley. To keep the defenders looking over both shoulders, he sent the Hasty Ps south to outflank the garrison by taking two prominent heights, Monte Tiglio and Monte San Giorgio. Major Kennedy left nothing to chance, arranging thorough reconnaissance, communications, support weapons, and artillery. The battalion began its march after dark on August 1 and by the following morning two companies had seized Monte Tiglio, finding the enemy weapons pits empty. All four companies then paused to size up

the next step, an assault on the southern escarpment. 'D' company entered the intervening valley to lure enemy fire, allowing the mortar crews and artillery spotters to locate the gun positions. One company scaled the undefended Monte San Giorgio to give covering fire to 'B' and 'C' companies in the culminating assault against the German paratroopers on Tower Hill. Late on August 2 Regalbuto was in Canadian hands.

Histories of the 2nd Brigade's battalions all describe the Salso valley as the most intractable terrain that the Canadians had to deal with in Sicily. The tracks northeast from Regalbuto expired before reaching the Salso river. There were no eastward roads in the broad, fertile valley floor, studded on its northern side by a series of peaks, knolls, and crags, some named, some numbered. Rifle companies had to go it alone until the engineers could get crossings over the Salso and create the semblance of routes for tanks or wheeled vehicles. Mule trains could carry heavy weapons and equipment, but the pace was slow.

The Edmontons were first into the Salso valley, heading for their initial objective at Hill 736, a height which dominated the junction of the Salso river and

William Ogilvie, *Mule train above a river bed* [CWM 19710261-4643]. The Canadians soon learned that mules provided the only suitable means of transport in the rugged, roadless terrain of Sicily.

its tributary, the Troina. Since the Adrano-Troina road ran beside the tributary, Hill 736 had to be captured to prevent the Germans from interfering with the Anglo-Canadian drive through the Salso River valley as well as with the parallel American advance down Highway 120. The Germans had quickly reoccupied the height after an Edmonton patrol found it empty on July 31. Between August 2-5 the Edmonton companies toiling over the rocky ground had to claw their way point by point up the slope before they were able to win the position. In the final attack, Lieutenant John Dougan was hit in both arms. Gripping his revolver in both hands, he led a charge over 300 yards of open ground to overwhelm the last of the enemy defenders.

The episode speaks for the hardiness of Canadian soldiers after five weeks in Sicily. The soldiers who dashed up these precipitous slopes were now a different breed from the unfit newcomers who needed some shaping up in the first days after the landings. The stamina of the Edmontons impressed an officer and war artist who walked up Hill 736 the next day. Both had to stop four times just to catch their breath.

The Seaforths showed the same toughness in assisting the Edmontons at Pt. 344, a feature sitting up on the forward slope of Hill 736, and in taking their own objectives along the spur that tapered out in the corner of the Troina-Salso junction. The Patricias then secured a crossing over the Troina, setting the stage for the next push to the Simeto river. Simonds put together a strike force composed of Three Rivers tanks, Seaforth infantry, and SP guns (named "Booth Force" after its commander) to thrust ahead to a spur along the western bank of the Simeto. The speed and combined arms of Booth Force worked to great effect in breaking through the wilting defences west of the river. In an attack surveyed by the British and Canadian commanders from on high at Centuripe, the tanks carried the infantry past the Troina-Adrano road; after letting their passengers off, they "moved forward at best tank speed" to shoot up the enemy positions while the Seaforths steadily overcame the parties of enemy infantry along the spur. Late afternoon saw the Seaforths consolidate their hold on the spur, while the Edmontons secured their objective at Monte Revisotto. On the morning of August 6, the Patricias brought the

William Ogilvie, *Mountain stronghold, Hill 736* [CWM 19710261-4640].

operation to an end when they took the last height at Monte Seggio.

With the way now clear for the 78th Division, the Canadians were withdrawn into reserve for a well-earned rest. They played no further part in the battle for Sicily, which went on for another ten days. British and American forces continued to push the Germans into the northeastern corner of the island, without defeating them decisively or cutting off their retreat. By the time that the British and Americans converged at Messina, the Germans had slipped across the strait to safety in southern Italy, there to await the Allies' next move.

"Less than two months after its initial landing First Canadian Infantry Division left the island behind it, and the vivid drama of the short summer campaign became only a memory as the longer and grimmer struggle on the Italian mainland developed." Fleeting as the memory of Sicily may have been, the Canadians had made a contribution to the campaign out of all proportion to their numbers. Their arduous 120-mile trek from Pachino to the Simeto had taken them further than any other British division, and they had borne the brunt of the Eighth Army's battle in the two hard weeks of fighting from Leonforte to the doorstep of Adrano. They had earned high praise from their Eighth Army commanders and comrades, and they had won the grudging respect of the Germans for their fighting spirit and skills. More importantly, from a national perspective, they had also won Canada's first victories of the Second World War.

Hill 736 and the adjacent Point 344 (lower right), seen across the Salso Valley from the SS 121.

A Canadian convoy proceeds along Highway 121 through the centre of Regalbuto. Today a monument to the suffering and resistance of the Italian people during the German occupation stands close to the spot where the motorcycles are parked.

William Ogilvie, *Preparing a diversion at a railroad bridge near Regalbuto*, Sicily [CWM 19710261-4691].

The same site today, photographed not far from the place where Ogilvie depicted the sappers of the 3rd Field Company, Royal Canadian Engineers, hard at work as they prepared a crossing for tanks and vehicles over the Salso River.

The Tour

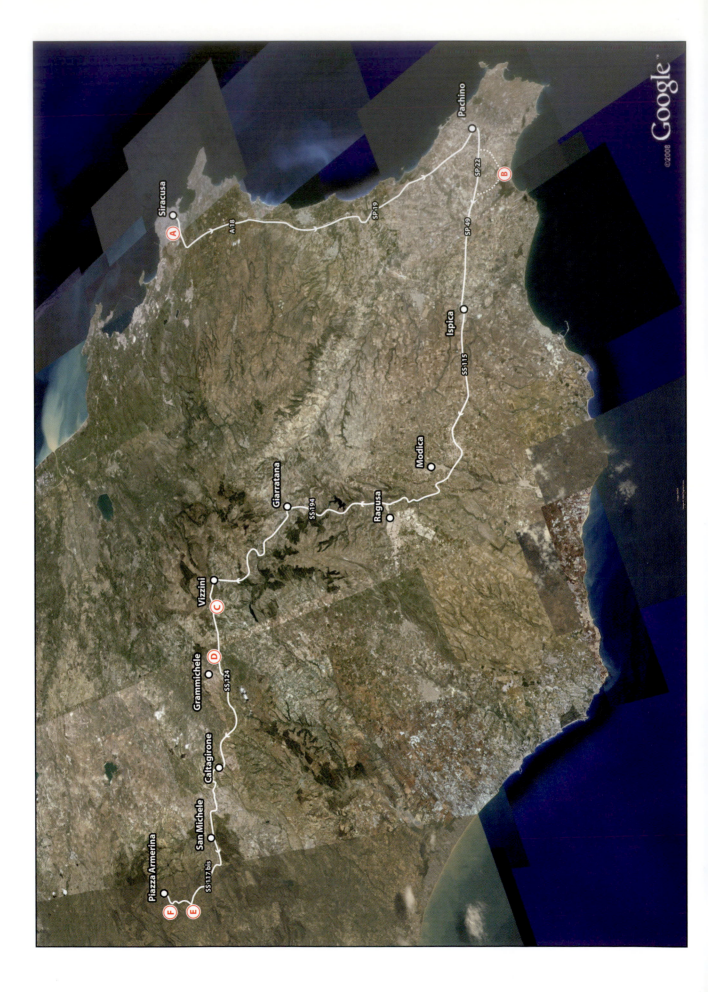

Tour 1 - From Pachino to Piazza Armerina: July 10-17, 1943

A If your journey takes you to southeastern Sicily, Siracusa should be one of your stops. The town and the adjoining harbour at Ortigia are full of history, and you will want to visit the Syracuse War Cemetery, located on the SS 124 beside the communal cemetery. Most of the 1,059 burials resulted from the 13th Corps' landings and first battles in the Plain of Catania. The disaster that befell 1st Airlanding Brigade on the night of July 9-10 is grimly evident in Plot V where many of the burials are unidentified. Lack of landmarks, high winds, inexperienced pilots, and flak combined to bring 69 gliders down in the sea, and scatter 59 over twenty-five miles of rocky countryside. Just twelve landed near the objective at the Ponte Grande bridge (which carries the SS 115 over the Anapo river south of Siracusa). Graves bearing the dates July 13-14 testify to the heroism of the 1st Parachute Brigade at the Primosole Bridge (south of Catania where the SS 114 crosses the Simeto river) and of the 3rd Commando at the Malati bridge near Lentini. From Siracusa you can take the SS 124 west to Vizzini, and then through Grammichele and Caltagirone to the SS 117b and Piazza Armerina where the first tour begins.

B Should you wish to visit the Pachino peninsula, turn south on the A18 to head for Noto and the SP 19 for Pachino. Bear in mind that the landing zones at Pachino are a far cry from the Normandy beaches saturated with monuments and museums. A monument to 1st Canadian Division was dedicated in 1991 at Marza, a small community on the western edge of the Canadian landing zones, and a plaque commemorating the Canadian assaults has now been placed on "Roger" beach, but apart from these there is not a great deal to see. One veteran of Operation Husky, Syd Frost, could hardly reconcile the awesome spectacle of the invasion with the unprepossessing site he visited only a few years later. The limestone spit known as Le Grotticelle is a useful marker dividing "Sugar" from "Roger", and you can make out the tips of the Costa dell'Ambra at Punta Castellazzo and Punta delle Formiche. What were barren, sparsely settled flats in 1943 have been largely built over, so the perspective of the attackers is now lost. You can complete the first leg of the Canadian advance by taking the SP 22 to Ispica where you will pick up the SS 115 for Modica and Ragusa, and then the SP 194 north through Giarratana to Vizzini.

Syracuse War Cemetery

Sicily Tour

Sicily Tour

Italian Campaign expert and battlefield tour guide Lee Windsor describes the Canadian landings on the beaches near Pachino [Matt Symes].

C The features that played into the hands of the Germans become clear at Vizzini. The town extends along a ridge overlooking all approaches, an ideal setting for a handful of defenders to hold up a column of tanks on the narrow, looping roads and an infantry brigade strung out over the hilly terrain. 51st Highland Division spent two days of often disjointed fighting before taking the town, only to find the defenders gone.

D You can follow the Canadians along the old Highway 124 (entwined with the railway line) to Grammichele where a similar scenario was re-enacted. From the raised eastern edge of the town rearguards of the Hermann Goering Panzer Division opened fire on a mixed vanguard of Hasty P infantry and Three Rivers tanks, pinning them down in the saucer-like plain. The alacrity of the response, however, seems to have surprised

The town of Vizzini, overlooking all approaches and ideally suited to the delaying tactics employed by the Germans as they fell back to their main defensive positions.

the Germans. The destruction of the lead Sherman on the outskirts prompted the crew of a Bren-gun carrier to charge the enemy .88 before it could reload. As though on a training exercise, the infantry companies used fire and movement to enter the town from three directions. In less than three hours the place was cleared and the advance resumed. Heavy bombing had driven the Germans from the next town, Caltagirone, and the Canadians met little opposition until they turned north on Highway 117.

The heights dominating the highway (today the SS 117bis) south of Piazza Armerina [Matt Symes].

(E) Five kilometres south of Piazza Armerina, the SS 117b makes a pronounced curve and passes through a valley overlooked by two large hills to the right of the highway. This was the place where the Edmontons ran into machine gun and mortar fire from the heights on either side of the road. 'A' company was sent to clear the Germans from the hill immediately beside the road (where the now elevated portion of the roadway comes to an end), 'B' company to the bulkier eminence a little to the east, while British SP guns and artillery fired in support. The Germans, here identified as detachments of the 15th Panzer Grenadier Division, gave 'B' company "a terrific battering" before slipping away. This was the last time that the "lean, sun-tanned professionals, superbly arrogant" would disengage so obligingly.

(F) Piazza Armerina is famous for the mosaics housed in the Villa Romana della Casale west of the town. The Hotel Ristorante Mosaici da Battiato is close by the museum which is well indicated on roadsigns in and around the town. The historical centre features a Baroque cathedral and an Aragonese castle, both worth a visit, so allow time for these monuments before you set forth on the tour of the Canadian battlefields.

Major William Pope and Lieutenant-Colonel Ralph Crowe of the Royal Canadian Regiment check a map in Piazza Armerina, 17 July 1943. Pope was to die the next day near Valguarnera, Crowe a week later outside Nissoria [PA 132777].

Sicily Tour

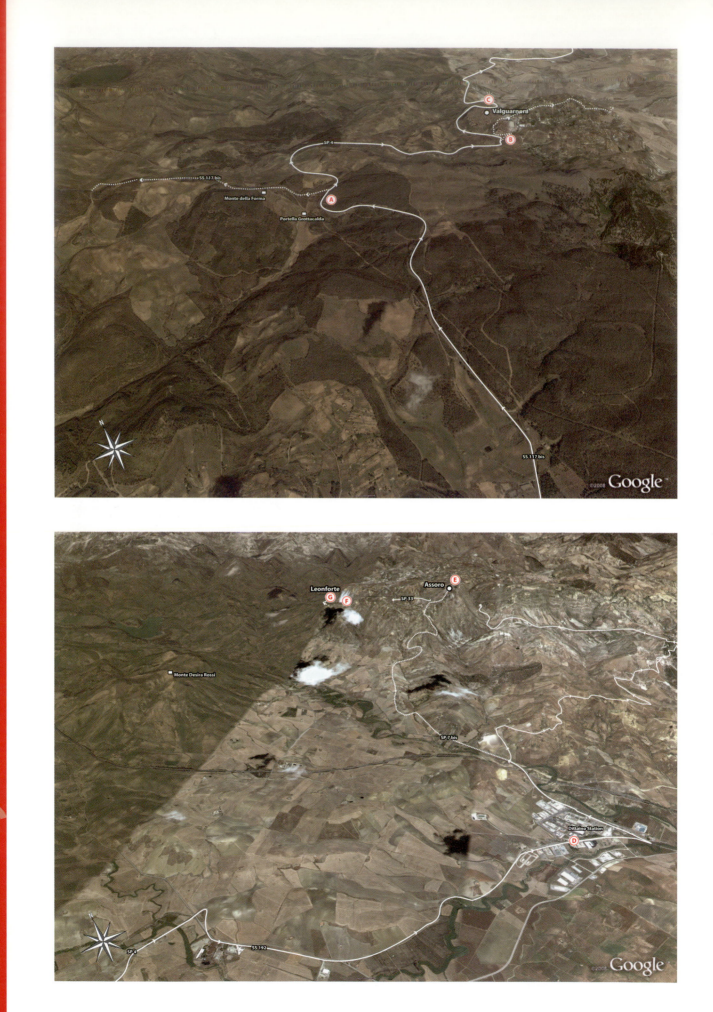

Tour 2 - Piazza Armerina to Leonforte: July 10-17, 1943

This tour leads you through the areas where the Canadians met their first concerted opposition in the Sicily campaign. The first portion of the route, from Piazza Armerina into the Dittaino Valley, keeps to the highway, but the second portion, covering the dramatic actions at Assoro and Leonforte, will require careful concentration as you find your way along the local roads. Take your time, and if in doubt, simply follow the signs for Assoro.

Heading north from Piazza Armerina take the SS 117b for Enna and Valguarnera. Note the SP 288 on your right which marks the starting point the Hasty Ps' right hook on the night of July 17-18. Following the 3rd Brigade's advance, stay on the SS 117b until it joins the SP 4. Note that the road system around Valguarnera has now been reconfigured. The highway has been relaid on the smoother contours of the old railway line, but the features that shaped the Canadians' first real battle in Sicily are still worth observing.

(A) As you approach the junction of the SS 117b with the SP 4 you will come around a C-shaped bend in the road, known as "Beginner's Hill" or "The Horseshoe" to the Carletons. Turn west onto the 117b and then pull into the secondary road immediately on the left. You are in the Portella Grottacalda, with Monte della Forma rising steeply on your right. This was the scene of the Van Doos' initiation to battle in which five soldiers earned medals. The right-flank advance by the Carletons aimed for the high ground astride the SP 4 about a kilometre northeast of the place where you are standing. If you wish, you can drive a little further down the 117b, noting the corridor to Enna on your right and the sharply angled bend in the road opposite the high ground won by the West Novas. Return to the SP 4 and turn left for Valguarnera.

(B) As the SP 4 bears to the right towards Valguarnera you will be entering the area where the 1st Brigade actions took place. At the last bend where the road turns north, just in front of the town, you will see a road leading to the right through the eastern side of Valguarnera. This was the road used in 1943 – the modern SP 4 now carries traffic west around the town – and you may wish to pause here momentarily. 'D' company of the Hasty Ps set up a roadblock near the first bend where they destroyed over a dozen German vehicles after 'B' company stirred up the enemy in the elbow bend in the old road. If reading Farley Mowat's account has given you a particular interest in the Hasty Ps' action east of Valguarnera, take the road into town where it becomes Via Mazzini and follow it to the piazza where you will see Via Angelo Pavone. Take this road east for two kilometres, at which point you will see the high ground to your right where 'A' and 'C' companies ambushed the German convoy proceeding along this east-west lateral.

The chief of police of Valguarnera, flanked by British and Canadian officers, reads the regulations now in force following the town's liberation from Fascist rule [PA 1967-052 22853].

C The route north from Valguarnera follows a slightly different course than it did in 1943. As the SP 4 descends from the town you will see a place to pull over on your right. Stop here for a few minutes to see what the soldiers of the 2nd Brigade saw as they headed down into the Dittaino Valley. Directly ahead, the peak of Assoro stands a head taller than the massif. Ten kilometres to the east you will see the spire of Agira; nearly seventy kilometres away the mass of Mount Etna rises over eastern Sicily. Except for alterations in the road system, very little before you has changed.

Continue along the SP 4 towards the causeway and buttonhook back to the SP 192. You will be heading left (east) for Stazione Dittaino, but note that the 1943 version of the SP 192 carried the Princess Louise Dragoon Guards (the divisional reconnaissance unit) westwards to meet the Americans at Enna while the Seaforths and Patricias angled northwest along a track (today the SP 7/a) leading to Highway 121 and Leonforte. From the causeway you will see ahead on your left a large crag, just beyond the Autostrada. This is Monte Desira Rossi, captured by the Patricias on July 20.

D Head along the SS 192 for Dittaino Station (Stazione di Dittaino in local parlance) and watch for signs indicating the road for Assoro (initially the SP 57). Now part of an industrial zone, Dittaino Station was the base for 1st Brigade's assault on the town. Here you have a choice of routes. Take the SP 57 to the railway trestle and then go right on SP 7bis (7/b) for Assoro. Soon you will come to a fork – the road on the left is the one that Lieutenant-Colonel Sutcliffe and Captain Cockin were reconnoitring when they were killed by an .88 shell. It is also the road that the 48th Highlanders followed as they pressed up to the western side of Assoro in relief of the embattled Hasty Ps. If you take this steep, winding road you will certainly appreciate the difficulties in approaching Assoro from this direction.

The road bearing right is signed for Nissoria. It takes you on a wide arc to another road bearing left (just before the hamlet of San Giorgio) that eventually brings you into full view of the eastern cliff face at Assoro. This route gives you a ground-level appreciation of the terrain through which the Hasty Ps made their night march. Be advised that this road is not well maintained and that some portions will require careful driving. It can be done safely enough in good weather. As you pass by the cliff face, note the deep ravine ringing the southeastern corner and the ledges on the side formed by the centuries of terraced cultivation. Goat paths allowed the heavily laden infantrymen to traverse the ravine, and the ledges supplied a rough staircase for their ascent.

E Make your way around the mountain towards the road into Assoro, taking notice on the way of the graceful viaduct that once carried the local rail line (now disused) across the gorge. You will of course want to go up to the summit to see where the Hasty Ps held on for dear life through the day of July 22. Signs inscribed Castello or Parco urbano point the way to the castle. Brace yourself, for the drive through the narrow, one-way streets of Assoro is enough to make you think that the Hasty Ps took the easy way after all. If driving does not appeal, you can park in the piazza by the church and walk up. The site is open between 9:00 am and 5:00 pm, although opening times vary with the season. Mid-morning is a safe bet.

A plaque has now been placed on the crest to honour the Hastings and Prince Edward Regiment. It includes a map outlining the battle for Assoro. From this vantage point you will enjoy a panoramic view for miles in every direction. If you look back over the town below you will see a saddle-shaped gully, where the 48th Highlanders fanned out after their long climb to take control of the T-junction on the western edge of Assoro. Beyond are two knolls. The one closer provided the base for the Edmontons' assault on Leonforte after errant shells hit the Seaforths' 'O' group assembled on its neighbour to the west. Look north along the massif where the German batteries were positioned, and note the road between the escarpments which furnished the German escape route from Assoro. To the northeast you can see the small town of Nissoria nestled in the shallow bowl just in front of the ridge further to the east. The prominent feature beyond the town's northeastern corner is Monte di Nissoria. The ridge line formed the first hurdle in the Canadian drive on Agira – the castle-topped cone profiled against Mount Etna. The view to the east replicates the Olympian perspective of General Simonds and his staff as they monitored events from the crest by the castle ruins.

The eastern slope of Assoro. In Lord Tweedsmuir's words, "the mountain was terraced and always above was a tantalizing false crest, which unfolded to another crest when one approached it. It was forty sweating, tearing minutes before we stood on the top beside the shell of the great Norman castle and realized that we had achieved complete surprise … we had control of a vantage point from which we could see for fifty miles."

The ruins of the castle on the summit of Assoro. As recently as 2006, ration tins and bits of equipment left by the Hasty Ps were found in the area around the castle walls.

Captain J.A. Fraser, one of the Canadian staff officers and photographers who went back over the Sicily battlefields in July 1944, is surrounded by local children as he surveys the landscape from a crag near the crest of Assoro [e000945236].

(F) Head back down and follow the signs west for Leonforte. As you approach the bridge where the SS 121 crosses the ravine, take the time to stop (there is a layby on the left-hand side of the road shortly before the bridge). The setting is exactly as it was in July 1943. Note the long reverse curve and the deep ravine that made an attack on Leonforte so difficult. As you go from the bridge to the curve where the road enters the town, spare a thought for the brave actions of Major Arthur Welsh of the 90th Anti-Tank Battery who managed to get two six-pounder guns across the ravine to knock out a machine gun and a tank blocking the entrance to the town. Major Kenneth Southern of the Royal Canadian Engineers had previously taken a fighting patrol up this stretch of the road to forestall the German tanks and infantry gathering for an attack against the sappers working at the bridge.

(G) The central avenue in Leonforte is the Corso Umberto I, a one-way thoroughfare running north-south. You will enter the town on a parallel one-way in the opposite direction, so it is probably best to go a few blocks and find a place to park. Walk to the circular Piazza Margherita which offers a good perspective up and down the Corso, and take some time to stroll through the southern (and oldest) part of Leonforte. Founded in 1610, Leonforte is a typical città di fondazione (new town) of its era, laid out along a strong linear axis and endowed by its patron Nicolo Branciforte with a Palazzo and Cathedral at the head of the town, and with La Gran Fonte on the terrace at the town's southern tip. There are fine views towards Enna from this point.

At the height of the battle the Edmontons coalesced in the maze of streets around the Piazza Margherita. The relief column rounded the turn into the town and made its way straight down the Corso until the destroyed German tank blocked the way just beyond the Piazza. The Patricias went forward on foot, clearing out the enemy around the railway station and tracks on the northeastern edge of town (since demolished, but the site is still known as Piazza Stazione) and taking the fight into the high ground beyond. If you stand on the western side of Leonforte you will see to the northwest the knoll where Private Cousins knocked out the two German machine guns.

After exploring Leonforte, make your way to the SS 121 which exits the town at its northern end for the short drive to Nissoria where the next itinerary begins.

The hairpin turn and bridge site where the Royal Canadian Engineers built a temporary crossing to allow Canadian tanks and reinforcements to move into Leonforte [Matt Symes].

A present-day photo showing the view south from the Piazza Margherita along the main street in Leonforte (the Corso Umberto I) where the battle for the town raged during the night of July 21-22 1943.

Street scene in Leonforte shortly after the battle showing the Corso as it runs north from the Piazza Margherita [e008300281].

Mortar platoons from the Princess Patricias check their equipment under the gaze of the townspeople gathered in the Piazza Margherita [e008300282].

Tour 3 - Leonforte to Agira:
July 23 - 28, 1943

The northern end of Leonforte projects further along the SS 121 than it did in 1943. As you leave the town you will see on your right the SP 33, formerly a track, which the 48th Highlanders followed to the SS 121 before turning right for the T-junction with the SS 117 just ahead. The Canadians sent patrols north along Highway 117 to establish contact with the Americans as 1st U.S. Division began its drive along the parallel Highway 120.

A As you approach Nissoria, take note of the town's setting and the ridgeline beyond where the highway passes through. You will be diverted to a one-way road that rejoins the SS 121 at Nissoria's eastern tip. Keep an eye out for signs to San Giorgio, and take that route if you wish to have a look at a couple of landmarks in the RCR battle. On the southern edge of the town, the communal cemetery occupies a knoll where 'A' company came under fire on the way to the high ground ahead. It was from this point that the RCR companies began to feel their way around the German flank. Continue towards San Giorgio. The land here has been heavily reforested, but as you draw near the village you will notice the defile on the left where the RCR companies slipped around the southern end of the ridge. It is not possible to see much more at this point, given the state of the labyrinthine farmtracks, so head back to Nissoria and proceed to the intersection with the SS 121.

You may make one more quick side trip here to gain some appreciation of the obstacles in the Canadians' way. Cross the SS 121 onto the road leading north. As it curves

"The Red Schoolhouse" (photographed in 2006).

right, you will be facing the ridge known as "LION," where you will see a red building on the right (beside a yellowish modern building) – the abandoned Casa Cantoniera (formerly a depot used by the highway supervisor) which was the Red Schoolhouse. If you continue along this road you will come beneath the rounded peak of Monte di Nissoria. The 48th Highlanders crossed the gully you are in to attack three points between Monte di Nissoria and the Red Schoolhouse. The topographical odds against them, to say nothing of the enemy mortars and machine guns along the crest, are plainly evident from this perspective.

B Return to the SS 121 and turn left. The highway slices through the ridge and passes the Red Schoolhouse on the left about a kilometre out of town. Just past the building there is a road on the left (Contrada Montagna) that runs along the northern part of the "LION" feature. At the fork, bear left to go up to the top of Monte di Nissoria. From here you will have a commanding view over the terrain through which 1st and 2nd Brigades fought on the way to Agira. Directly ahead, the ground dips and rises to form the next ridge line known as "TIGER" which the Seaforths captured in the early hours of July 27. Look at the terrain and picture the infantrymen, blanketed in dust and smoke, inching forward in the dark of night to feel out the enemy positions.

C On the short drive along the SS 121 to Agira, take note of the 90° bend to the left through a wooded area. This marks the outer fringe of the objective designated as "TIGER." In the final bound to Agira, the Seaforths' 'A' and 'C' companies swept diagonally across the highway ahead towards Monte Fronte, while 'D' company set out from here towards Cemetery Hill. Agira has spilled down the slope to cover what was open ground in 1943 and you will want to keep your eyes on the road at this point where six routes converge on the eastern edge of town. Bear left to stay on the SS 121 where it passes the walled communal cemetery and winds round the northern side of the town. Watch on the right for a street marked Via Palazzo and signs indicating the way to the Castello and venture into the upper part of the town. The signs guide you to a promenade where you can park and walk the rest of the way up to the ruins of the castle.

Sicily Tour

The ridgeline that marked the "TIGER" objective as seen from Monte di Nissoria. The summit of Agira is visible just above the crest.

This 1944 photo shows the "GRIZZLY" objectives as seen from "TIGER." The photographer, Sergeant J.E. Deguire, noted that he took the photo from an observation post used by 1st Brigade during the attack on Agira [e008300291].

(D) Agira belonged to the network of Norman outposts radiating out from Enna during the 11th century when the fortifications on the crest were first built up. The fragments of the castle, however, date from the era of the famed monarch Frederick II. From the summit of Agira, practically the whole Canadian campaign in Sicily lies within view. To the southwest you can see, tracing the landscape from left to right, Dittaino Station, the citadel of Enna, and the fortified crest of Assoro. To the west is Nissoria – look south of the town to see the valley where the RCR companies slipped around the German defences on "LION." Closer to Agira, the stages of the final push are easily identified. Down to the left is Monte Fronte, and just to the right of the main road is the hill where the communal cemetery can be seen amidst the stands of pine trees. The round top of Monte Crapuzza rises a little further to the right.

Looking south you will see another dome, Monte Gianguzzo, immediately to the left of the highway (the SP 21). This point was taken on three successive nights (July 25-27) by the 1st Dorsets of the 231st Brigade as they aided and abetted the Canadian attacks by thrusting up the road from Raddusa to Agira. Until the Canadians took Agira, however, the Dorsets had to retire from Monte Gianguzzo to avoid being hit by artillery fire supporting the Canadian efforts. The 1st Hampshires likewise gained and left Monte Campanelli three nights in a row; this objective lies east of Agira, a little to the north of the Canadian war cemetery which you should be able to make out across the causeway – it is the patch of green framed by pine trees in the corners. Further on you can see Regalbuto and the Salso river valley where the final Canadian battles took place on the approaches to Mount Etna.

You can refresh yourself at the Ristorante-Pizzeria Belvedere not far from the promenade (there are plenty of

The view from the castle ruins crowning Agira back over the scenes of the Canadians' hardest battles in Sicily -- Assoro, Nissoria, and the physical features that marked the stages of the advance to Agira.

signs pointing the way). Otherwise, make your way back down to the SS 121, heading east for Regalbuto. This will take you to the Hotel Castel Miralago, with a stop at the Agira Canadian War Cemetery.

(E) The burial ground was chosen by Canadian graves registration officers shortly after the campaign ended. It is fitting, in this remote, serene place, framed against the majestic backdrop of Mount Etna, that the headstones face Agira, for nearly half of the 490 soldiers buried here died within sight of the ancient town. The architect, Louis de Soissons, adorned the site with an impressive entrance way, using stonework and features reminiscent of Italian villas, and laying pebbled mosaics imitative of Roman styles to evoke the ancient past. The only exclusively Canadian burial ground of the Second World War, Agira is small enough to be the most affecting, for here you will recognise many names and note

the concurrence of many dates and regiments in connection with each stage of the Canadian battle from Pachino to Adrano.

Continue along the SS 121 towards Regalbuto. The next itinerary starts at the Hotel Castel Miralago which you will find on the left of the road just before you reach the town. It is a good place to pause for a meal or for a stay before embarking on the last tours.

The mosaic terrace and the stone stairway leading to the burial ground at Agira Canadian War Cemetery.

Tour 4 - Through the Dittaino Valley:
July 24 - August 3, 1943

Although not as detailed as the previous itineraries, the drive along the route followed by 3rd Brigade takes you through a scenic interior region of Sicily where the principal change has seen the rural populace move to the cities or emigrate. The empty landscape and abandoned dwellings betoken the hardships of Sicilian life that struck observers so forcibly in 1943. This part of the tour perhaps brings you closest to the Sicily which the Canadians knew.

If you are starting from Regalbuto, take the SP 60 di Calabro (signed for Catenanuova) which leaves the SS 121 between the town and the Hotel Castel Miralago. Go all the way to the T- junction with the SP 59. About a kilometre to your left is Monte Peloso, secured by the West Novas after the capture of Catenanuova. For the moment turn right and follow the lateral road to the SP 21. As you draw near this road you will have marvellous views of Agira to the north. You will remember that the SP 21 was 231st Brigade's axis of advance as it supported the Canadian drive on Agira from the west.

A Turn left (south) on the SP 21 and follow it beneath the Autostrada to the Raddusa-Agira rail station where you will join the SS 192. The rail station was the starting point for the 3rd Brigade advance to Catenanuova which you can follow by turning left (east) on the SS 192. This was the only route through the Dittaino Valley in 1943, running alongside the river and the rail line. A few kilometres on, you will see a sign for Libertinia, the base from which the West Novas set off to pass around the southern side of Monte Scalpello. A little further on is Stazione Libertinia, where the Van Doos gathered for their assaults against Monte Santa Maria and the northern slope of Monte Scalpello.

B The corridor between the two features takes shape as you see Monte Scalpello looming up on your right – the buildings visible on the summit belong to the sanctuary of Santa Maria del Rosario, founded by three eremitical monks in 1524 and still visited on feast days. To the left, across the river, you will see the sprawling dome of Monte Santa Maria, twice taken by

An abandoned farmstead in the Dittaino Valley, one of many revealing the postwar exodus from Sicily's harsh interior to the towns or abroad.

the Van Doos in the preliminaries to the assault on Catenanuova.

C Follow the SS 192 as it crosses the Dittaino and bear left on the SP 74. On your way over the bridge note the banks and riverbed where the Canadian sappers had to grade a crossing under enemy fire so that tanks and vehicles could come up in support of the West Novas and Carletons fighting in the hills beyond the town. On entering Catenanuova, you may wish to make a short sidetrip west along the Via Palermo which will lead you out to Monte Santa Maria. While 'C' company under Captain Paul Triquet (of Casa Berardi fame at Ortona) overran the dazed defenders on Santa Maria, 'D' company worked its way north to Hill 204 along the stream bed which you can see winding like a green ribbon along the eastern base of the hill. After you return to the town to pick up the SP 23b for Regalbuto, you will pass the feature on the left of the road at the 3-kilometre mark.

D As you head north on the SP 23b, note the T-junction on the left where the lateral road you took previously runs by Monte Peloso. The last 3rd Brigade actions took place east of the SP 23b. The West Novas struck northeast from Monte Peloso across the road to the low ridge they called "Whistling Hill"; from here they advanced into the costly encounter with the paratroopers on Monte Criscina, four kilometres east of the road. Heavy machine guns on Whistling Hill covered their withdrawal to the little hamlet of Rosamarina, a placename (no longer used) indicating the little cluster of houses on the left of the road at the 11-kilometre mark.

E Some of the key sites in the next itinerary will appear as you complete the drive to Regalbuto. The road winds between two hills, the dome of Monte Tiglio on the left, and Monte San Giorgio, the higher peak to the right. Note for future reference the deep cleft dividing Regalbuto on its southern side. The high point on the left, marked by radio masts at the tip of the Regalbuto ridge, is Monte Santa Lucia, and the loftier summit across the gorge is Tower Hill. All these landmarks will figure prominently in the final itinerary which begins back at the Hotel Castel Miralago.

William Ogilive, *Disabled German light tank and line of prisoners* [CWM 19710261-4513].

A view of Agira from the south, showing the route taken by 231st (Malta) Brigade in its advance from Raddusa.

The Dittaino Valley, with the Raddusa-Agira railway station visible on the right. This was the starting point for 3rd Brigade's advance towards Catenanuova.

The dome of Monte Santa Maria with Monte Scalpello in the background. The line of trees marks the little streambed which 'D' company of the Van Doos followed towards Hill 204.

Tour 5 - From Regalbuto to the Simeto River:
July 29 - August 6, 1943

A The best place to begin is the parking lot on the east side of the Hotel Castel Miralago. From here the landmarks in the battle for Regalbuto are easily identified. Down to the left you can see the dome of Monte Serione and the communal cemetery where the 48th Highlanders squared off against the German tanks and infantry opposing their advance along the low ridge skirting the northwest corner of the town. To the right, the Regalbuto ridge, bravely taken and held by the Devonshires, rises in a hog's back alongside the highway. Further to the right you can distinguish Monte Tiglio in front of the square top of Monte San Giorgio where the Hasty Ps outflanked the town and moved in to clear Monte Santa Lucia and Tower Hill.

B There are two ways into Regalbuto. The SS 121 goes through the town. If you take it, keep an eye out for a white cross on the slope of the ridge just on the edge of town. The monument was placed in honour of the Devonshire Regiment's achievements on July 30-31. On the base are listed the names of the regiment's officers killed in the Sicily campaign. Follow the SS 121 into the town, past the little jog to the right and park near the large school facing the cleft on the south side of town. If you wish to follow the RCRs around the southern side of the ridge, take the second right off the SS 121 and follow this road (Via G. Filippo Ingrassia) around into the town where it joins the main street near the school.

C From the street in front of the school you can get a good view of the cleft where the RCRs clung to the slopes beneath Tower Hill. A soccer pitch now lies in the curve of the horseshoe formed by the ravine, but you can walk through the narrow streets on the west side where the RCRs tried to work their way through a serious physical obstacle not shown on their tactical maps. 'D'

William Ogilvie, *Bombed House and the Church of St. Agatha* [CWM 19710261- 4435].

The monument to the Devonshire Regiment on the western edge of Regalbuto.

company reached the lip of the ravine on the east side, followed by 'A' and 'B' companies, but all three found themselves pinned to the gully's sides when enemy fire denied further progress. Of the day-long ordeal Strome Galloway wrote, "The day passed slowly and the sun blistered down. Our thirst and hunger were maddening. For fourteen hours we stayed there without a drop."

Before leaving Regalbuto, take a few minutes to look around. By the end of the battle, the town was an empty, flattened wreck. Afterwards, a transport officer proceeding through the rubble-strewn streets described the inhabitants returning to their homes "as a pitiful sight, dirty, ragged, frightened, and apparently half-fed. They were accompanied by the town's canine population and hordes of flies". The misery of the civilian population, and the harshness of the German occupation of Italy, would increase as the campaign went on. To appreciate something of the memory of the war in Italy, go into the small garden overlooking the gorge where there is a statue of a schoolchild. Below on the plinth, a poem is inscribed. It was written by Piero Calamandrei, a scholar and jurist who made no secret of his opposition to the Fascist regime, in response to a remark made by Albert Kesselring. The German supreme commander in Italy was tried after the war for his part in the Ardeatine Caves massacre of March 1944, in which 335 Italian civilians were shot outside Rome in retaliation for the killing of ten German soldiers by the Resistance. Kesselring was initially condemned

to death, but the sentence was commuted and he was released from prison in 1952 on the grounds of age and ill health. An unrepentant Nazi to the end, he declared that the Italians should build him a monument to honour his services to their country. Calamandrei's reply begins, "You will have the monument you ask from us Italians, comrade Kesselring, but of what stone it shall be built is for us to decide," and ends by stating that it should be made not with the blackened ruins of destroyed villages or the earth covering the victims of a cruel occupation, but –

> *...only with the silence of the tortured*
> *Harder than any boulder,*
> *Only with the rock of the pact*
> *Sworn among free men*
> *Who of their own free will rallied*
> *Out of human dignity, not hatred,*
> *In their determination to redeem*
> *The shame and terror of the world.*
>
> *On these streets, should you wish to return,*
> *At our posts you will find us,*
> *The living and the dead,*
> *Arrayed in the same steadfast ranks*
> *Around the monument*
> *Called, now and forever,*
> *RESISTANCE.*

A 1944 photo showing the inhabitants of Regalbuto rebuilding their shattered town [e008300295].

William Ogilvie, *Returning Refugees* [CWM 19710261-4720].

The remainder of the tour, covering the advance through the Salso valley, presents a choice between two routes. The road that follows 2nd Brigade's advance along the northern edge of the Salso river is little more than a track in many places and should not be attempted in bad weather. This more taxing path does heighten appreciation of the terrain and the key episodes in the last days of the campaign, but it is not for the faint of heart or the weak of suspension. The path of least resistance keeps you on the SS 121, which runs along the massif overlooking the Salso valley and affords a good view, if at a distance, over the scenes of 2nd Brigade's operations.

(D) 1) The easy way: Take the SS 121 east from Regalbuto until you come to a crossroads about five kilometres on. Stop here and look across the Simeto valley to see the knob of Point 344 in front of the imposing Hill 736. The Edmontons and Seaforths found the approach from the southeast easier and so carried on towards the Troina tributary before wheeling back up to the high points they were to take. While the Edmontons dealt with Hill 736, the Seaforths cleared the ridgeline projecting into the corner formed by the junction of the Simeto and the Troina. Across the Troina you will see Monte Revisotto, and about three kilometres to the right, Monte Seggio.

From this crossroads you can take the road leading north across the Simeto to join the track followed in the harder itinerary – bear right along the path followed by Booth Force to the SS 575 north of Carcaci. Otherwise, stay on the SS 121. Thirteen kilometres from Regalbuto you have the option to go up to Centuripe and enjoy a tremendous panorama over the last stages of the Canadian battle. The eight-kilometre uphill drive is not difficult but there are many sharp bends where local drivers may not be expecting to meet oncoming cars. Stay alert at the curves and do not stray into the middle of the road. Centuripe from the air resembles a starfish extended along the ridges emanating from the town centre. Difficult to approach, much less capture, it took hard fighting by the 38th (Irish) Brigade before 78th Division could move through to its thrust line along Highway 121 to Adrano. From this mountain village Simonds, Leese, and the artillery spotters monitored the Booth Force operation on the far side of the Salso valley.

(E) From the Centuripe road, it is three kilometres along the SS 121 to the Simeto. You will pass over the Salso where the road now passes over a new bridge that replaced the adjacent structure marking the site of the crossing in 1943. Just before you reach the Simeto, however, you will see the SS 575 on your left. Take this road towards Carcaci and the scenes of the Booth Force action which are outlined at the end of the harder itinerary.

(F) 2) The hard way: From Regalbuto, take the Via Garibaldi to the southern exit from the town. The road runs by the communal cemetery and Monte Serione along the gully reached by the 48th Highlanders. Just past the cemetery the road bends to the right. Follow the sign for Sparacollo and stay on this road (SP 69 di Monreale, a track in 1943 which the Seaforths' carriers used for about a mile until it gave out) all the way to the Salso river. Go over the bridge and pause on the other side.

Back, to the right of the road, you will see a railway bridge. The 3rd Field Company of the Royal Canadian Engineers graded the approaches to this bridge so that tracked vehicles could get over the riverbed; the sappers also smoothed a path for wheeled transport across the boulder-strewn riverbed beside the railway, where on August 4 the war artist Major William Ogilvie sketched them at work from about the point where you are now standing. Their efforts made possible the assembly of tanks and SP guns for use in Booth Force.

(G) Continue to the T-intersection, turn right, and go rattling along the Seaforths' line of advance alongside the Edmontons who were higher up on the left. When you come to a narrow passageway beneath the railway line, look left (north) to see the main features, Hill 736 and the lower outpost of Pt. 344, and the spur running parallel to the Troina streambed, just ahead. When you come to the crossing over the Troina, pause again to note key points. The Patricias secured a ford above the railway bridge to prepare the way for Booth Force on August 5. Almost due north is Monte Revisotto where the Edmontons finished the job of taking the two commanding heights over the Troina-Adrano road on August 5-6. From the Troina, the Three Rivers tanks of Booth Force sped ahead as far as this road (now the SS 575), which you will come to at the end of your bumpy track. Just before reaching the road, the Seaforths leapt off the tanks to assault the ridge line rising up to Monte Seggio, northeast of the track and the SS 575.

The Salso Valley, seen from its western end where the Canadian push towards Adrano began.

Turn right and follow the road as far as Carcaci. A lane now leads into the place – the main road once ran through but was diverted around the settlement after malaria emptied the place of its inhabitants. Its history goes back to the beginnings of the Norman period in 1061, and it preserves a fascinating shell of a mediaeval community complete with castle and church (the castle is not open to visitors at this time but may reopen at a later date). This little pinprick on the map fell to the London Irish as 78th Division closed up to the Simeto on the Canadians' right. On the way between Carcaci and the Simeto bridge you will see spanning the river a stately acqueduct (built in the 18th century and considered one of Sicily's wonders). North of the aqueduct, the Van Doos put the last feather in the Canadians' cap, thanks to the failure of the radio sets. A patrol under Lieutenant Yvan Dubé was reconnoitring the approaches to Adrano when orders came for all Canadian units to pull back to the western bank of the Simeto so that 78th Division could move through. Dubé, "par suite d'une panne de radio", did not receive the message and led his men into Adrano, finding the place deserted and the German army in full retreat west of Mount Etna. His report suspended preparations for an all-out bombardment and assault upon the town and allowed 78th Division to hasten its steps in pursuit of the enemy.

(H) The Canadian tour concludes at the Simeto bridge. If you are continuing east from here, you should think of visiting the war museum in Catania (Museo Storico dello Sbarco in Sicilia 1943, with information about location and opening times available at museosbarcosicilia@provincia.ct.it). You should make a point of visiting the Catania British War Cemetery, southwest of the city near the airport. In long rows over two thousand British soldiers lie at rest, many of them from 13th Corps, whose bitter struggle in the Plain of Catania is largely explained by a glance north towards Mount Etna. The lower slope rises like a series of shelves overlooking the plain. From this dominating position the Germans could hold out indefinitely against frontal attacks, as they did for four weeks until the Anglo-Canadian divisions of 30th Corps finally punched through to Adrano and rendered the German defences south of Mount Etna untenable.

Catania British War Cemetery, with the city of Catania to the right and Mount Etna in the background.

Agira Canadian War Cemetery as photographed in 1944 [e008300297; inset DND ZK-828] and as it appears today. Note the trees planted around the burial ground to check soil erosion and to retain water, and the construction of an impressive entrance way with its limestone walls and mosaic patios.

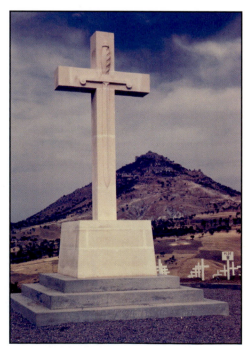

Right: The Cross of Sacrifice placed at the central axis of the cemetery, and the cone of Agira in the background [DND ZK-829].

Introduction

Southern Italy

While the Canadian role in the Sicily campaign was drawing to a close near the town of Adrano, Winston Churchill was aboard the Queen Mary en route to "Quadrant," the first of the two Allied conferences held in Quebec City. This was the British Prime Minister's second trip across the Atlantic in 1943 and, as during his visit to Washington three months before, his purpose was to secure an agreement on future strategy. During the "Trident" conference of May 1943, Churchill had pressed President Franklin Roosevelt to accept his proposal to exploit the capture of Sicily by invading the Italian mainland. Convinced that Italy offered a direct avenue of attack into the southern flank of the Reich ("the soft underbelly"), Churchill envisioned the prompt capture of Rome, followed by an advance into northern Italy where the Allies could launch a thrust through the Alpine passes into either France or Austria. The Americans, however, had insisted on limited action against Italy. They suspected that Churchill and the Chief of the Imperial General Staff, Field Marshal Sir Alan Brooke, were trying to expand the Allied commitment in the Mediterranean. General George Marshall, Roosevelt's indispensable and single-minded military adviser, was willing to countenance an operation to seize Naples and open the way to Rome, but he took the same line regarding Italy that he had in the discussions over Sicily. Operations in the Mediterranean must not delay or impede the principal effort against Nazi Germany. In return for American agreement to the invasion of Italy, Marshall extracted a promise from the British that the cross-Channel assault (soon to be designated as Operation Overlord) would proceed by May 1 1944 with 29 American, British, and Canadian divisions positioned in England by early 1944. Seven of these were to be transferred from the Mediterranean. The discussions at "Quadrant" ended in a compromise whereby the Americans accepted Churchill's ambitious plan to "knock Italy out of the war" and to engage as many German divisions as possible in Italy; on the other hand, the British had to accept the relegation of the Italian campaign to secondary importance once "Overlord" commenced.

The Allied staffs planned two major landings in Southern Italy. The first, codenamed Operation Baytown, called for an attack by the Eighth Army across the Strait of Messina into the toe of Italy. The second, codenamed Operation Avalanche, would bring U.S. Fifth Army (including British 10th Corps) ashore at Salerno, south of Naples. Meanwhile, the changing political situation in Italy presented opportunities and complications to the Allies. The invasion of Sicily had dealt the death blow

Coming ashore on the mainland of Italy. After making the short crossing from Sicily (dimly perceptible in the background), large transports and a flotilla of DUKWs – the invaluable amphibious vehicles that solved the problem of maintaining the flow of supplies to armies in the initial stages of an invasion – pour their cargoes onto the beach near Reggio di Calabria, September 3, 1943. Thanks to the Allies' total command of the air, Operation Baytown proceeded without hindrance from the enemy.

to Benito Mussolini's Fascist dictatorship. The Duce was deposed on July 25 and replaced by a provisional government headed by Marshal Pietro Badoglio. Although outwardly loyal to the Axis partnership, Badoglio and King Victor Emmanuele II were contriving to have Italy capitulate and re-enter the war on the Allied side. Rightfully fearful of German retribution, Badoglio sent emissaries to the Allies requesting that Allied forces be despatched to Rome to secure the capital. It was beyond the Allies' power to do so, however, and by the time Italy announced its surrender on September 8 1943, the Germans, who had been anticipating developments along these lines, had rushed troops into the country to seize control and to counter the Allies well south of Rome. Badoglio and the King fled south (via a minor port on the Adriatic called Ortona) and left a vacuum of authority which the Germans quickly filled. Any hope that the Allies might quickly reach Rome evaporated when the Germans occupied Italy and decided, after some strategic wrangling of their own, to force the Allies into a grinding attritional struggle against a succession of defensive lines strung across the peninsula.

Background

The Canadian government played no part in the formulation of Allied strategy concerning Italy. As the host at Quebec City, Prime Minister Mackenzie King was present for photo ops with Churchill and Roosevelt, but he "accepted the position that the higher direction of the war was exercised by the British Prime Minister and the President of the United States." The Canadians received notice that their troops in Sicily were scheduled to take part in Operation Baytown, and Lieutenant-General Kenneth Stuart, Chief of the General Staff, gave formal approval on August 17.

The soldiers of 1st Canadian Division and 1st Army Tank Brigade began to prepare for their part in Baytown on the basis of lessons learned in Sicily. The key to success in battle was skill in the use of ground for attack, defence, and the defeat of the enemy's immediate counterattacks to regain lost positions. Training exercises concentrated on "fieldcraft, siting of weapons, camouflage, cover, observations, use of compass, and map-reading." Infantry

William Ogilvie, *Field Artillery on the move*, October 1943 [CWM 19710261-4533].

battalions were to organise and train sniper and scout platoons while emphasizing the role of 3" mortar and Bren gun carriers in supplying firepower. Each brigade was urged to deploy the Saskatoon Light Infantry platoons of 4.2" mortars and medium machine guns well forward. The terrain of Italy made heavy mortars, with a range of 3,000 yards, crucial weapons in "softening up or smoking an objective" while their accuracy required "a high standard of drill and discipline." The Vickers machine gun, "one of the best weapons in our armoury," worked most effectively when used in enfilade with a section of two guns as the fire unit. Training in infantry-tank cooperation was also stressed, and everyone was reminded of the need for strict anti-malarial precautions.

All agreed that the terrain dictated the methods to be used in conducting an attack. Once the fire plan was in place, rifle companies should make themselves more elusive targets by advancing dispersed on a wide front. They were also to avoid the crests of ridges. The best approach was to stick to defilade and shadow, and, if in doubt, to take the long way around. Above all, it was imperative to keep moving once the attack started. Stopping was a sure way to bring enemy mortar fire down upon you.

While the soldiers trained, Major-General Guy Simonds and his staff developed detailed plans for the Canadian division's part in "Baytown," a curiously limited operation. Simonds outlined the division's task at a conference held on August 24. The Canadians, together with 5th British Division, were to capture a beachhead on the mainland side of the Strait of Messina "so that the straits are free for the use of our own shipping." The secondary purpose was to "draw enemy resources against the beachhead" to assist in the success of the Anglo-American landings at Salerno scheduled to take place once the beachhead at Reggio di Calabria had been secured.

Simonds was probably aware of Bernard Montgomery's unhappiness at the minor role assigned to the Eighth Army. The hero of El Alamein was not used to being a supporting actor, and once it became clear that Mark Clark, the American general in charge of Operation Avalanche, would fight the main battle, Monty "sulked in his caravan" and allowed Baytown to develop as a set-piece assault landing with an elaborate and unnecessary bombardment of an undefended coast. Few resources were allotted to the pursuit of the enemy who were known to be planning to withdraw from the southern tip of Italy.

Simonds decided to plan for a pursuit role as well as the bridgehead battle. He selected 3rd Canadian Infantry Brigade for the assault landings with 2nd and 1st Brigades to follow. He warned his brigadiers that once ashore he would not hesitate to pool the limited transport available "to make one brigade mobile, stripping the assault brigade to a skeleton to do so." Unfortunately, the loss (to an enemy submarine) of a shipment of Canadian-made four-wheel-drive vehicles had not been made up, and the Canadians were forced to rely on borrowed two-wheel-drive lorries that had seen "lengthy service in Africa." The staff of 1st Canadian Division were grateful for the loan, but they made it clear that when new Canadian trucks arrived they would return the British trucks promptly.

The march inland begins. Canadian troops and vehicles passing through Terreti, September 3, 1943 [e008300305].

History

Messina to Potenza and beyond:
September 1943

The battalions of 3rd Canadian Infantry Brigade had not played a major role in Operation Husky – the invasion of Sicily – in part because they had performed poorly in pre-invasion training. The campaign in Sicily provided an opportunity to fix some problems and improve the level of company training, but Simonds was still unhappy with Brigadier M.H.S. Penhale who in Simonds's judgment was too cautious and too old for active command. Penhale's preparations for the landings on the Italian mainland seemed well organised and the rehearsal went smoothly, but on D-Day itself (September 3 1943), there was much confusion. Fortunately, there was little resistance. The German 29th Panzer Division began a staged withdrawal and the Italian coastal division quickly surrendered.

Simonds ordered the Canadians to advance inland beginning on D+1. Unfortunately, he had to follow orders to secure the mountainous core of the "toe", the Aspromonte, instead of advancing along the coastal road. The decision to send Canadian troops into this incredibly difficult country made no military sense whatsoever. The roads – often little better than tracks – wound their way up barren hills in a series of switchbacks. The enemy was bound to withdraw from the area or surrender once the "toe" had been bypassed. As a result, the Canadian battalions sent into the mountains were in no position to respond when General Sir Harold Alexander urged the Eighth Army to push north "regardless of administrative (logistical) consequences." Montgomery ignored this plea. He instructed the Canadians to move south to the coast where they were to pause and build up resources.

Major A.T. Sesia, the divisional historical officer, kept a detailed diary in September 1943, and his entries capture the character and flavour of this strange interlude. "3 September: The night was pitch-black and no lights were visible from the enemy shore … At precisely 0345 hours our artillery barrage opened up … The noise from these guns kept the night air reverberating with a steady roar. Every now and then tracer shells would cross the

Charles Comfort, *Passo di Fratemorto* [CWM 19710261-2155].

water in a horizontal line of flight. Firing along fixed lines they guided our landing craft to their proper beaches … The barrage lasted until 0530 hours. Here and there fires were burning along the enemy coast and every now and then the sky would be lighted up in a greenish blue glow indicating a direct hit … All morning the news from the fighting front was good. Practically no opposition was encountered … We drive off the beach into Reggio di Calabria … another air attack took place and enemy fighters shot up the town and dropped bombs too close for comfort … Thus did I, for the first time, set foot on the land of my forefathers. Reggio was deserted … the people had fled to the hills, the population had dwindled from 170,000 to 20,000 when the invasion of the mainland appeared imminent.

"4 September: As we drove through the town, I saw that the city, possessing so many beautiful buildings, was so battered by our air bombing and shelling that there was hardly a building left unscathed … Apparently all day yesterday considerable looting went on. It is probably difficult to differentiate between looting and scrounging … the generally accepted view is that looting is sheer vandalism, in scrounging one takes what one needs to render more efficient the prosecution of the war."

His diary entry for September 5 notes that patrols had reached far inland in all directions, but had not yet contacted any Germans. It also states that the enemy had carried out extensive demolitions to hinder the advance. "The mountains in this area form part of the Aspromonte chain and rise in height up to 6,000 feet. We are therefore pretty well confined to tracks and roads…

"6 September: Immediately upon leaving Reggio we climbed the high hills by way of steep winding roads … After darkness had fallen we drove without lights up and down hair-raising grades and sharp bends. In a way it was a godsend that we could hardly see more than five or ten feet ahead of us since we knew we were driving along a road with no guardrail above ravines ranging in depth from 600 to 2,000 feet. To add to the discomfort it commenced raining and soon developed into a downpour … Apparently the Germans have withdrawn … and the Italians refuse to fight…

"7 September: We pushed off at noon … a slow trip due to demolitions and diversions. Warning signs such as 'Danger! Use four-wheel drive if you want to see Canada again!' Heavy guns are firing to the northwest of us from naval craft which are supporting the landing of 231st Brigade (on the west coast of the "toe")."

The entry for September 8 notes that Sesia spent most of the morning at Operations Command. "The situation on our front is fluid … our forward troops have in no way made contact with the enemy … Italy has surrendered. This news did not surprise me, as it was evident since the invasion of Sicily that the Italians were not prepared to continue the war. What lies in state for 1 st Canadian Division is now a matter of conjecture until such time as a plan is worked out.

"9 September: The situation up front is still unchanged. No actual contact with the Germans has been made … the BBC announced this morning that a large

Engineers of the 1st Field Company put a Bailey bride over a blown crossing between the towns of Terreti and Straorini [PA 193871 / e008300304].

British and U.S. force has landed near Naples. We packed up early this morning, proceeded in convoy 57.2 miles … surrounded by awe-inspiring scenery … At every town, village and hamlet the inhabitants stood outside their homes to cheer us."

That afternoon Montgomery ordered the Canadians to pause and regroup as the "build up across the straits from Sicily is very slow…". The next day, D+1 for Operation Avalanche, the landings at Salerno, General Sir Harold Alexander, who commanded both Eighth British and Fifth United States Armies, urged Montgomery to "maintain pressure against the Germans so that they cannot remove forces from your front and concentrate them against Avalanche." Avalanche had been planned in the context of negotiations for an Italian surrender, with 82nd U.S. Airborne seizing and holding Rome while Fifth U.S. Army advanced swiftly from Salerno to Naples. However, Allied intelligence analysts failed to understand Hitler's determination to rescue Mussolini and hold onto as much of Italy as possible. The men of Fifth U.S. Army had cheered the news of Italy's surrender as the convoys approached the beaches but were shocked by the speed and intensity of the German reaction to the landings. Four of the five German divisions in southern Italy were moved to Salerno to seal off and destroy the bridgehead. The fate of the Anglo-American forces hung in the balance for the next six days without any involvement on the part of Eighth Army.

"We fought and marched 300 miles in 17 days, in good delaying country against an enemy whose use of demolition caused us bridging problems of the first magnitude," wrote Montgomery in his memoirs. "Fifth Army did their trick without our help – willing as we were."

C.J.C. Molony, the British official historian of the Italian campaign, suggests that Montgomery did try to implement Alexander's orders to maintain pressure, but "administrative difficulties rather than the enemy" prevented a rapid advance. Molony's description of these difficulties is worth quoting: "Transport is the bugbear of armies and, like original sin, is the everlasting occasion of accusation, railing, disturbed consciences, and censorious, vain preachings. In modern armies there is at once too much transport and not enough. The chief causes of this condition are elaborate weapons greedy for huge quantities of heavy ammunition, high military social standards which require for the urban man in uniform much food and medical care, and in the urban man himself a capacity to endure hardship far lower than that of the harshly nurtured man of Minden, of Sebastopol, or of First Ypres. Yet it is idle to look for a Golden Age of hard-bitten sparseness in an imaginary past. In 1914, the kind eyes of 5,592 horses, the transport of an infantry division of that day, rested on a marching crocodile of men only 18,000 strong but 15 miles long, and staff officers 'swore terribly in Flanders'. Their successors have done the same there and elsewhere for kindred reasons."

Few observers believe that transport problems were responsible for Montgomery's failure to press the advance with any sense of urgency. None was communicated to the Canadians who spent four days resting near the beaches of the Adriatic before beginning an unopposed advance along the coast towards Taranto, the scene of the famous torpedo-bomber attack upon the Italian fleet in 1940. Taranto, located on the heel of the Italian boot, was captured without opposition by 1st British Airborne. The Canadians were thereupon ordered to turn inland and advance to Potenza, a road and rail junction fifty miles east of Salerno.

Alexander had given Montgomery a direct order on September 17 to "secure Potenza"; in turn, the latter assigned the task to the Canadians. Simonds thought his instructions were too vague and wrote to General Sir Miles Dempsey, the corps commander, noting that he was "not quite clear as to whether it is now desirable to make 'military noises' in that direction as quickly as I can, or whether we should lie up until the whole division is ready to advance." Simonds proposed to move quickly on Potenza "unless I hear from you to the contrary." He met with Lieutenant-Colonel Pat Bogert, the commanding officer of the West Nova Scotia Regiment, and told him that he was to take charge of a motorised battlegroup made up of a squadron of tanks from the Calgary Regiment, engineers, a battery of self-propelled artillery, a platoon of medium machine guns from the Saskatoon Light Infantry, and a troop from the divisional anti-tank and anti-aircraft regiments. A company from 9th Field Ambulance, Royal Canadian Army Medical Corps, completed what became known as BOFORCE. The advance north commenced on the morning of September 18.

An account of the challenges faced by BOFORCE, based on the West Nova Scotia Regiment's war diary, reads: "At 0500 hours in the early morning of 19 September, A company … moved forward to the blown bridge just west of Laurenzana to cover the operations of the engineers who were constructing a diversion. When these were in hand, A company moved forward on foot followed by Lieutenant-Colonel Bogert's command party and D company. The force was now moving along a steep defile at the confluence of the Fiumara d'Anzi and the Fiumara Camastra, both with dry but substantial river bottoms. Scarcely a mile ahead of the column, German sappers blew a crater in the road and another diversionary operation was necessary.

"Shortly afterwards, as A company rounded the bend overlooking the river beds, the bridge carrying the road across their junction was blown and the enemy demolition squad opened fire on the leading troops. Fire from three-inch mortars was immediately brought down, an enemy lorry was hit and the Germans hastily withdrew. Lieutenant-Colonel Bogert placed tanks at the head of the column as soon as they could be brought forward in order to frustrate for the future any similar activity on the part of enemy demolition parties. Just before reaching Anzi, another blown bridge was discovered and D company went forward on foot while the remainder of the battalion closed up in troop-carrying vehicles. Anzi was entered at approximately noon and three German vehicles, which were visible on the road beyond, were engaged by the leading tanks and withdrew hurriedly. In addition to the increasing number of craters and blown bridges and culverts, the road from Anzi onwards was studded with Tellermines." (A Tellermine was one of forty different types of German anti-tank mine. Various kinds contained from ten to twelve pounds of explosives.)

Potenza, the largest city in the region of Basilicata, was founded in pre-Roman times as a settlement on the slope of a south-facing ridge above the Basento river. The poor agricultural land had led to the depopulation of the rural areas; however, Potenza had developed as a regional centre around its 12th-century cathedral. Beginning on September 13, the Allied air forces began attacks on the city's railroad yards and road junctions. Potenza, crowded with refugees from the Salerno battle area, was targeted by Allied heavy bombers on six consecutive days, and much of the city was destroyed in these attacks with heavy loss of life.

The decision to bomb Potenza was just one example of the lack of overall strategic direction of this phase of the Italian campaign. Allied intelligence, based on Ultra and other sources, had reported German intentions "to throw the Allies back into the sea" at Salerno. By September 14, however, the crisis in the beachhead was ending, and Eighth Army was supposed to be on the move north. The first hints of a German withdrawal were noted on September 17, but no one ordered the Allied air forces to cease attacking a town or the railway yards that the Allies would soon need.

The Germans had planned to hold Potenza with a regiment of 1 st Parachute Division, but orders to withdraw to a new line left the town in the hands of a company-sized battle group instructed to stage a delaying action. Historian Lee Windsor, who has studied the battle for Potenza and walked the ground, describes the initial attack by the rifle companies of the West Nova Scotias as one that "sacrificed the stealth of a footborne approach for the speed of using trucks." Unfortunately, mines blocked the approach and eliminated all hope of surprise. Two West Nova companies were pinned down in the dry riverbed and the advance stalled. When the Canadians mounted a second attack, using artillery, armour, and an additional infantry battalion (the Van Doos), the German paratroopers carried out their orders to withdraw. Canadian doctors treated sixteen wounded Germans as well as twenty-one Canadians. The real tragedy of Potenza, however, lay in the number of civilian casualties, estimated at over 2,000, including several hundred dead.

The aforementioned Major A.T. Sesia (the division's historical officer), reached Potenza on September 21. "The city itself," he wrote, "lies sprawled partly on the height immediately north of the river and on the northern bank of the river itself … at the immediate approaches to the town there was considerable damage. The artillery and especially the air force had created huge craters … good cars were destroyed or burnt out and some were blown great distances by the force of exploding air bombs." While exploring the city, Sesia noted a huge group of civilians in front of a bakery where bread was being baked for the first time in ten days.

The German Tenth Army, responsible for the eastern

sector of the Italian peninsula, had despatched 1st Parachute Division to the Foggia-Manfredonia area to block the British advance along the Adriatic coast. The German divisional commander noted that the flat Foggia Plains "were particularly ill-suited for campaigning with the weak forces of this division" and that everything possible must be done to delay the Allied advance until more troops were available. In the event, the general need not have worried. Logistical problems and a lack of urgency at Allied headquarters led Montgomery to regroup his Eighth Army along the Ofanto River just twenty-five miles north of Potenza. The Canadians were told to secure Monte Vulture and the town of Melfi, but no further advance was anticipated until October 1.

The German high command also issued orders on September 22, instructing the soldiers of Tenth Army to adopt measures outlined in a directive entitled Exploitation of Italy for the Further Conduct of the War. This order demanded that "extensive use be made of the Italian male population for further military and economic purposes." Both civilians and soldiers were to

be conscripted for construction battalions and "extensive use" was to be made of conscripted drivers, mechanics and fitters "in order that the German soldiers may be freed up for fighting." Supplementary orders required the confiscation of material in the Naples and Foggia areas that might be of value to the German war effort, especially locomotives, rolling stock, and trucks. Material that could not be removed was destroyed. The Canadians were to witness one of the most dramatic examples of Hitler's scorched earth policy when a Princess Patricias' patrol reached Atella, a village south of Melfi. That is where the Germans destroyed a section of the Apulian Aqueduct, the major source of water for the Foggia area and the heel of Italy.

As the Germans withdrew to Foggia and began construction of a series of defensive positions collectively known as the Winter Line, 13th British Corps (1st Canadian and 5th British Infantry Divisions) settled into a comfortable routine. The 1st Division's war diary entry for September 29 reported "strong rumours that there is a war on," but nothing interfered with "putting on a sports meet in the middle of a campaign." The entry goes on to note that Major-General Simonds "has developed jaundice and had to be evacuated to hospital. This is a bad blow to the division as it appears we are about to enter our heaviest battles so far." After several days of "confinement" at divisional headquarters Simonds insisted on returning to duty. He did so, but was forced to enter hospital when the classic yellow jaundice symptoms appeared. Brigadier Chris Vokes became acting divisional commander in Simonds's absence, and he was to command during the first heavy fighting that the Canadians faced on the mainland of Italy.

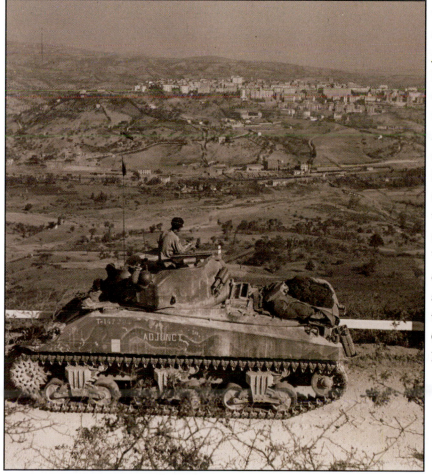

The crew of a Calgary Regiment tank survey Potenza from the south, September 20, 1943. The streambed of the Basento river winds in front of the railyard (centre) where the West Nova Scotias came under fire [PA 144103].

Southern Italy History

Pushing on to Campobasso: October 1943

Throughout the Italian campaign senior Allied commanders were privy to German intentions, courtesy of Ultra. By 1943, the code-breakers at Bletchley Park (the British government's communications headquarters located eighty kilometres north of London) were reading with minimum delays the messages encrypted by the Germans on their supposedly indecipherable Enigma machines. At both Eighth and Fifth Army headquarters, a select group of officers and non-commissioned officers – known as the Signals Liaison Unit – provided Generals Mark Clark and Bernard Montgomery with detailed reports on the enemy's plans and order of battle. The problem which Ultra could not solve in October 1943 concerned German strategy in Italy, since not even the Germans themselves had yet decided which course to pursue.

Field Marshal Erwin Rommel, of North African fame, argued that it was imperative to conserve German strength by withdrawing to a line north of Rome. Hitler at first agreed with this strategy. As a result, Generals Dwight Eisenhower and Sir Harold Alexander gave orders for an immediate advance upon Naples and the Foggia Plain. After a brief pause, the Allied armies would converge on Rome. The Allied commanders expected to encounter delaying actions, but they believed that the real fighting would take place north of Rome the following spring. On October 1, however, Ultra reported the gist of an interview between Field Marshal Albert Kesselring and Hitler in which the Führer reverted to character and ordered an active defence on the whole front, giving up as little ground as possible. Seven days later, Ultra was able to supply details of German plans to hold a winter position on the Bernhardt Line north of the Sangro River. Hitler's intelligence services had reported the movement of Allied troops out of the Mediterranean, leading him to conclude that the Allies were hoping to secure Rome

William Ogilvie, *Tanks moving towards Boiano*, Italy [CWM 19710261-4803].

as a political prize without a major investment of forces. This offered the Germans the opportunity to restore Mussolini (whom they had rescued from Gran Sasso in a bold operation) and retain control over most of the country with a small army relying on good interior lines of communication. The Italian theatre was allotted an inflow of eighteen supply trains a day from Germany and France, providing substantial stocks of ammunition, fuel, and food to supplement the large quantity of stores seized after the disbandment of the Italian army.

The Allied armies faced a very different situation. Montgomery repeatedly complained that Eighth Army lacked the supplies to wage an effective campaign. He warned the Chief of the Imperial General Staff, General Sir Alan Brooke, that both supplies and reinforcements would be required for an advance to Pescara since the "country in front of us is good defensive country and skilful demolitions would make the next advance slow." He then asked the key questions about the Italian campaign. "What do you want to do? I presume you want the Rome airfields, do you want Rome for political reasons, and to be able to put the King back on his throne? Do you want

Soldiers of 1st Canadian Infantry Brigade look at a "Canada Town" billboard in Campobasso, 21 October 1943 [PA 213690].

to establish airfields in the Po Valley? Do you want to drive the Germans from Italy? Are you prepared to have heavy losses to get any or all of the above?"

Montgomery offered his own view that it was "a mistake to drive the German forces from Italy." The Allies required only enough of Italy "to enable our air forces to be able to reach the southern German cities and the Romanian oilfields" and "keep the Germans guessing about our intentions." He warned that a great deal of fighting lay ahead if the Allies were to reach northern Italy. Brooke could provide no answer. He himself supported Churchill's idea of an aggressive campaign in Italy but he was equally aware of the Americans' unyielding insistence that Overlord be given absolute priority.

While this debate played out, Eighth Army began its attack on the Viktor Line with 78th British Division, made up of veterans of the Tunisian and Sicilian campaigns, advancing along the Adriatic coast. The 78th, known as the Battleaxe Division, was to be assisted by an assault landing behind enemy lines at Termoli, a small port north of the Biferno River. No. 3 Commando and No. 40 Royal Marine Commando, with the support of the Special Raiding Squadron, captured Termoli in the early hours of October 3. The commandos then handed the port over to 78th Division's 56th Brigade which arrived by sea. This well-executed manoeuvre should have forced a German retreat to the Sangro River some miles to the north, but the enemy instead decided to recover Termoli and sent 16th Panzer Division to counterattack. This put 56th Brigade in a precarious position since it had embarked without artillery or armoured support – this was supposed to arrive by land once the Biferno River had been bridged, but heavy rains slowed this task and left the lightly armed infantry under attack from powerful Panzer battlegroups. The commandos were recalled to help defend the perimeter, but the town could not be held for long unless a bridge allowing armour and anti-tank weapons to cross could be thrown across the river.

A British armoured regiment (County of London Yeomanry) was in action by October 4, but more armour was needed right away. The Three Rivers Regiment, which had landed at Manfredonia on October 1, was quickly sent to Termoli. The Canadian tanks crossed the Biferno on October 5 and engaged the enemy the next morning. The Three Rivers Regiment, commanded by

Canadian soldiers inspect a captured .88 gun that was part of the strongpoint overlooking the approaches to Motta Montecorvino [e008300308].

Lieutenant-Colonel E.L. Booth, had distinguished itself in Sicily, but this was to be its first purely tank versus tank contest. Their opponents of the 16th Panzer Division were equipped with Mark IV Specials, tanks with additional armoured skirting and a better gun than that carried by the Shermans. Success in such an action depended on the careful use of ground. In the course of the two-day battle the Three Rivers tank crews claimed ten enemy tanks destroyed and won wide praise for their role in forcing the Germans to withdraw from Termoli. After the battle, the commander of the 38th (Irish) Brigade, presented a shamrock pennant to Booth and told a British reporter that "it was the first time in the war that I have ever seen everything go exactly as it was supposed to … the tanks and infantry cooperated in complete textbook style – it was wonderful."

The repulse of the German counterattack at Termoli forced the enemy to pull back to the Sangro River. During their retreat, the Germans used delaying tactics to buy time for the construction of better defences. Enemy units received a directive outlining the use of "lines of resistance." Such positions were to be arranged by setting up strongpoints manned by small groups which could slip away at night if heavily engaged. No two lines were to be less than ten to twelve kilometres apart so that Allied artillery could not fire at the second position without

moving forward. These were the tactics encountered by the men of 1st Canadian Division during their advance from Foggia to Campobasso. Before handing over to Brigadier Chris Vokes, Simonds had outlined the plans

A Three Rivers Regiment tank in action near Termoli station, October 6, 1943 [e008300307].

Charles Comfort, *Canadian guns firing on German positions near Campobasso* [CWM 19710261-2251].

for this move.

Leading the way from the start line at Lucera was a strong vanguard organised around the divisional reconnaissance unit (the Princess Louise Dragoon Guards), a squadron of Calgary Regiment tanks, and a company from the Royal Canadian Regiment. They ran into the first enemy "line of resistance" at the village of Motta Montecorvino which the Official History describes as sitting "like a thimble on a pointed hill atop the first main ridge." Lieutenant-Colonel F.D. Adams, commanding the vanguard, decided to wait for the follow-up force led by the Calgary Regiment's Lieutenant-Colonel C.H. Neroutsos. The rest of the Calgary tanks and the Royal Canadian companies arrived, but most of the guns of the artillery field regiments remained stuck in traffic south of Lucera. Neroutsos elected to go ahead without proper fire support, only to find that the Germans paratroopers were able to drench the approaches with machine-gun fire which separated the Canadian tanks from the infantry. At that point, Neroutsos and RCR commander Lieutenant-Colonel Dan Spry decided to withdraw the tanks and prepare a staged night attack once enough artillery support

was available. A short, intense barrage was upstaged by a violent thunderstorm illuminated by lightning that outdid the gun flashes. The RCR companies following the barrage found that apart from a few rearguards the enemy had melted away to their next "line of resistance."

While the battle for Motta raged, a Princess Louise squadron probing the hill tracks west of the main highway, met with one of the most peculiar units in the Allied order of battle, Popski's Private Army. Major Vladimir Peniakoff, a Belgian-born, British-educated son of Russian émigrés, had been working in Cairo at the outbreak of the war. After initial adventures behind enemy lines with the Long Range Desert Group, Popski, as he was universally known, commanded No. 1 Long Range Demolition Squadron in its raids on German supply depots. After El Alamein and Tunisia, the jeep-borne force, now sporting official PPA shoulder flashes, was sent to Italy in September 1943. Within days the PPA was operating deep behind enemy lines, shooting up German convoys as they withdrew from Potenza and Bari. On September 30, Popski and his men, working their way north on the corps' boundary, were more than happy to join in an impromptu attack on a

German platoon positioned to provide flank protection to the strongpoint at Motta. The combined PPA and Princess Louise contingent swept over the position from the rear and ensured that none of the enemy got away to fight another day.

Meanwhile 1st Canadian Infantry Brigade continued north towards Campobasso along the centre line formed by Highway 17. The 48th Highlanders were assigned the next bound to Volturava. The regiment's historian comments that "the apparent tough nut of Volturava was easily cracked" because the enemy had chosen better defensive positions along the San Marco ridge north of the town. Fortunately, an independent battlegroup composed of the 48th's C company, a troop of Calgary Regiment Shermans, anti-tank guns, armoured cars, and the invaluable heavy mortars and machine guns of the Saskatoon Light Infantry, had threaded its way north along a parallel route east of Highway 17.

The battlegroup commander, Major Ian Wallace, realised the German paratroopers holding the high ground dominating the main road had neglected to occupy the even higher ground behind their position. Wallace got his lead platoon onto this feature and ordered the men to hold their fire until they could be reinforced. Several short, sharp artillery shoots drove the paratroopers back into their slit trenches until Brigadier Howard Graham could coordinate an attack involving the RCRs and the 48th. The preliminary barrage, however, fell short and the RCR companies were late, with the result that the formidable San Marco feature was attacked by just two 48th companies.

The Wallace battlegroup staged a risky raid on the enemy, using a single platoon and a troop of tanks. When the lead tank was crippled by a mine, Lieutenant Blair Eby and his men "flung themselves among the scattered German slits … with Tommy guns and Brens stuttering from every hip." The paratroopers panicked and abandoned their forward slope positions. When the RCRs attacked the village of San Marco that night, a well-aimed artillery barrage snuffed out the last German resistance. By morning the paratroopers were gone.

It was now 3rd Brigade's turn to take the lead against a new enemy formation, 29th Panzergrenadier Division. A first attempt to cross the Fortore River near the broken spans of the Ponte dei 13 Archi met with failure; but a cross-country march by the West Nova Scotias and the Carleton and Yorks compelled the enemy to give up Gambatesa, a town four miles beyond the river. The Germans disengaged, surrendering a series of hills and villages in an attempt to conserve manpower and to hold a new blocking position on Highway 17 at Jelsi. Both the Germans and the Canadians were suffering a steady stream of casualties, but the Canadians continued to press forward along hill tracks as well as the main road. The Van Doos and the West Nova Scotias overcame the defenders at Jelsi at considerable cost and pushed the enemy back towards Campobasso.

A Canadian anti-tank gun being positioned near Campobasso [e008300300].

To the south, 2nd Brigade had proceeded across the grain of country in a series of moves that tried the patience and endurance of all involved. Still outfitted in their light Sicily campaign uniforms, the soldiers were soon "dog-tired and wet" and often underfed. Nevertheless, "skill and persistence" paid off, and the enemy, who had cultivated a healthy respect for the Canadians and an amply justified fear of their artillery, decided to abandon Campobasso. Artillery proved decisive in the brigade's battle for Vinchiaturo, for when Brigadier Bert Hoffmeister's battalions were in position the enemy deemed it prudent to withdraw "to prevent heavy losses … from superior forces and artillery fire."

The next line of resistance, south of the Biferno River, turned out to be an unexpectedly difficult barrier to surmount. The villages of Orantino, San Stefano, and Mongagno, and peaks such as Monte Vairiano, had to be captured before Campobasso – slated for use as an administrative and rest centre – would be safe from enemy shelling. To this end, a series of sharp, taxing attacks were necessary. By October 21, this task was complete, but Montgomery's decision to employ 5th British Division in an advance to Isernia as a means of diverting enemy attention from a major offensive along the Adriatic coast required the Canadians to seize and secure a start line beyond the Biferno. Simonds, who had left hospital early to resume command of 1st Canadian Division, told his weary men that they were to "hit a good hard blow" at the enemy before the British attack got underway. The first phase, the capture of the village of Colle d'Anchise and the high ground labelled Point 681, fell to the newly rechristened Loyal Edmonton Regiment. Troopers of the Ontario Regiment, fighting their first battle on the Italian mainland, provided armoured support. The tanks had to wait until the engineers could construct crossings over the river, and the Edmontons were forced to give up part of the village when their PIAT guns (Projector, Infantry, Anti-Tank) were of no avail against the German tanks. Once the Canadian tanks arrived, however, the Panzer battlegroups withdrew. The last actions planned by Simonds in Italy were thus completed by October 27, and the next day 5th British Division launched its diversionary attacks, reaching Isernia on November 7. By this time the Canadians were enjoying a well-earned respite in Campobasso which for a time doubled as "Canada Town," a home away from home for the 1st Division.

Canadian troops move past the obstacles left by the retreating Germans in Castropignano [e008300301].

The Tour

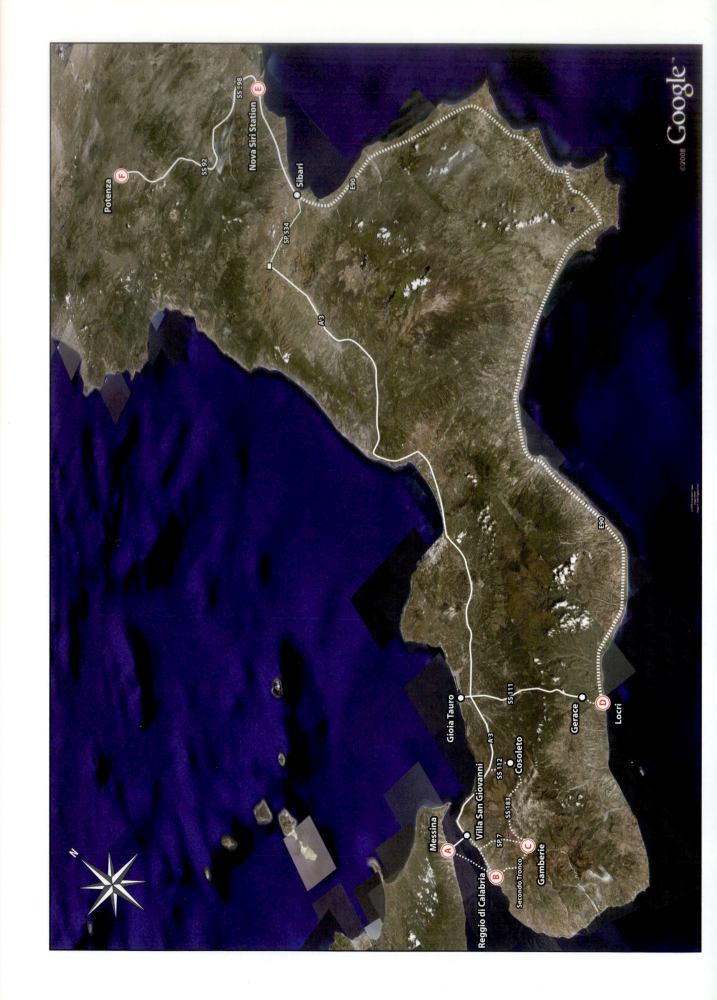

Tour 1 - Messina to Potenza: September 1943

Travellers crossing from Sicily to retrace the Canadian path through Southern Italy or to head for some of the region's best known sites (Paestum, Pompeii, Naples on the Tyrrhenian coast, or Lecce, Bari, Trani, Il Gargano on the Adriatic side) are in for a long haul. Not only are the distances formidable (about 450 kilometres to Potenza along the route outlined here, another 160 to Campobasso following the second itinerary), the roads twist and wind through mountainous terrain which in many places can be spectacularly beautiful but makes for slow going. Unless you keep to the Autostradas, it is impossible to move quickly through southern Italy; but this may also serve as an incentive to plan your trip in such a way as to appreciate an authentic part of Italy that few foreigners ever see.

A Someday in the future it may be possible to drive from Sicily to the Italian mainland over the world's longest suspension bridge. Until then travellers will have to use the ferries from Messina to Villa San Giovanni or to Reggio di Calabria. We recommend the shorter route, about twenty minutes, to Villa San Giovanni (as opposed to forty minutes to Reggio di Calabria). Ferries depart regularly from the harbour terminal located close by the train station. The route to the ferry terminal (follow the signs bearing the Italian word TRAGHETTI or marked with the ferry symbol) is well indicated from the A19 and other major roads leading into Messina. As you make the short crossing from Sicily to the mainland, bear in mind that the Germans brought more than 60,000 soldiers and all of their equipment across these waters in the last few days of the Sicily campaign. The failure of the Allies to prevent or disrupt this evacuation denied them a greater and more telling victory in the opening phase of the Italian campaign.

B No matter where you come ashore on the mainland, you owe it to yourself to visit the Museo Archeologico Nazionale di Reggio di Calabria (also known as the Museo Nazionale della Magna Grecia) which houses the magnificent Riace bronzes. These two figures of warrior-athletes were retrieved from the sea in 1972 and after years of cleaning were put on permanent display. Go to www.museodellacalabria.com for details on the museum's location and opening times (note that it is closed on Mondays).

1st Canadian Infantry Division crossed the strait between Villa San Giovanni and Reggio di Calabria and advanced inland to Gamberie. This took them into the Aspromonte, spectacular, rugged mountain country. Since little of military interest happened here, most tour groups bypass this area and head straight north along the A3 to the better known and more accessible battle areas around Salerno, close to the splendid temples at Paestum. If, however, you wish to retrace selected parts of the Canadian trek through Southern Italy, we offer two options.

The Strait of Messina separating Sicily (left) from the Italian mainland.

C The first is to drive through the Aspromonte to Gamberie. Two routes take you to the town, one being the SS 184 (also SP 7), followed by one of the British infantry brigades on the Canadians' left, which meets the A3 midway between Villa San Giovanni and Reggio di Calabria. The other is the Secondo Tronco Via Reggio Campi, used by 1st Canadian Infantry Brigade, which leaves Reggio di Calabria at the eastern edge of the town and eventually joins the SS 183 (also SP 3) leading to Gamberie. Both roads climb into the Aspromonte and introduce you to the topography of a region that impressed the Canadians by the contrast with Sicily. Instead of an arid, alien landscape, the soldiers found themselves on the move through mountainous terrain reminiscent of home with its thick coniferous forests and pine-scented breezes. From Gamberie you can follow the 48th Highlanders' route towards Cosoleto where you will bear left (west) along the SS 112 (SP 270) to reach the A3 on the coast near Bagnara Calabra.

This photo, taken in September 1943, portrays one of a never-ending series of switchback roads that gave the Germans plenty of opportunities to delay the Canadian advance [PA 193866].

This contemporary photo of Potenza was taken from the same place as the 1943 photo shown on p. 81 [Lee Windsor].

(D) The second, quicker route has you head north from Villa San Giovanni on the A3 and take the fourth exit, signed for Gioia Tauro, to pick up the SS 111 east for Cittanova, which was reached by the Edmontons and the Patricias approaching from opposite directions, and then on to Locri. There was no sign of 29th Panzer Division here or on the coast at Locri where "an unrestrained celebration greeted the Canadians and the news of Italy's surrender."

(E) From Locri the drive along the spectacular coastal highway (the SS 106) to Nova Siri Station on the Gulf of Taranto is a daunting 350 kilometres. You will see a part of Italy visited by very few North Americans, but it all adds up to a long day. The alternative is to turn back on the SS 111 after a brief stop in Gerace where the largest cathedral in Calabria stands over an especially lovely village. Have a cappuccino and return to the A3 and follow it north to the SS 534, direction Sibari, and from there make the short drive along the coastal highway to Nova Sira Station. Carry on past this point to meet the SS 598 where you will turn left (west) to meet the SS 92 after thirty kilometres.

(F) BOFORCE reached Potenza in 1943 by using the SP 104 and the SS 92, winding roads through scenic countryside that will test the driver's endurance on endless swithbacks. Your passengers, if not in the throes of car sickness, will marvel at the views but unless you find a place to pull over the driver had best concentrate on the road. As ever, stay alert, keep to the right, give way to speed demons, and do not count on oncoming drivers to be expecting you. Once you approach Potenza, take note that the West Nova Scotias' battlefield is now partially obscured by the new highway, but some of it can still be seen on your right as you enter the town on the S92. There are several good hotels in Potenza should you wish to make an overnight stop here. The *Vittoria*, south of the river, and the *Grande Albergo*, in the city centre, are your best bets.

Infantrymen of the West Nova Scotia Regiment riding on a Calgary Regiment Sherman tank during the BOFORCE advance to Potenza [PA 177155].

Southern Italy Tour

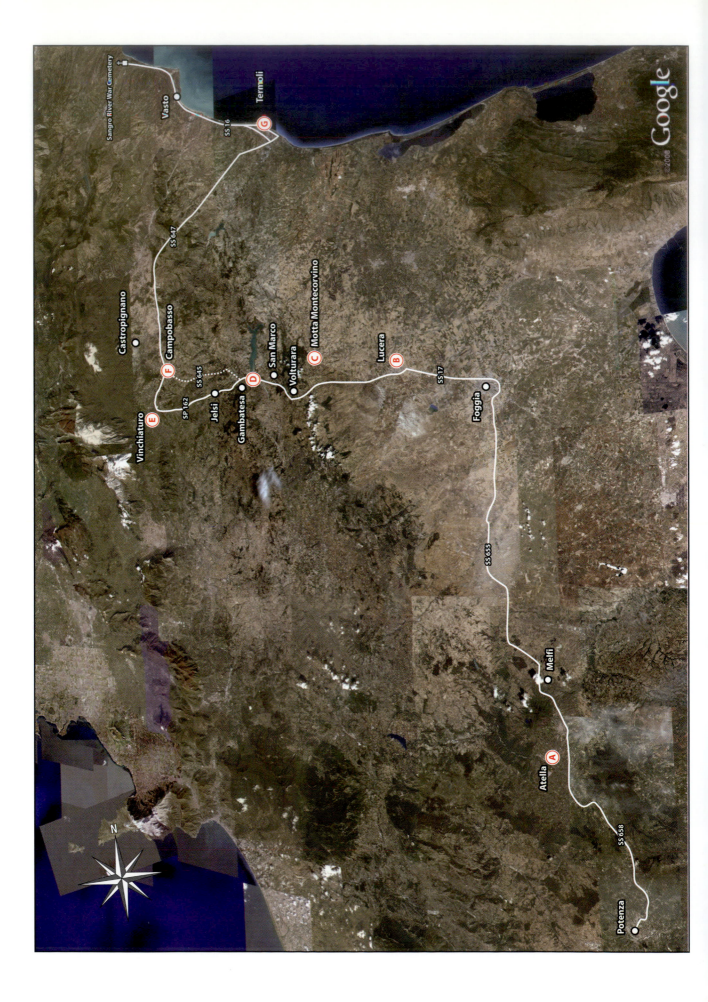

Tour 2 - Potenza to Campobasso: October 1943

(A) The next stage of the journey can be completed in several hours, but with stops along the way it will occupy most of the day. There was a series of short, sharp clashes on the road to Melfi, particularly at Atella where the Patricias ran into a blocking force of paratroopers. You can visit the Castello di Lagopesole, just south of Atella, to gain the same perspective over the area which the soldiers had in 1943. You may also wish to pause in Melfi which the Patricias and Princess Louise Dragoon Guards liberated on September 27.

(B) The Canadians moved briskly through Foggia to Lucera which was to become a Canadian base for the remainder of 1943 and well into 1944. The landscape here is open and windy, dotted by numerous modern windmills. There are several good hotels and a vibrant mediaeval town to explore.

(C) Campobasso lies less than a hundred kilometres from Lucera on the S17. Your first stop, Motta Montecorvino, is a walled village atop a peak in the Daunia mountains. The RCRs, accompanied by Calgary Regiment tanks, fought their first battle on the Italian mainland along the approaches to Motta Montecorvino, and you should make a point of consulting Colonel Strome Galloway's first person account on the Royal Canadian Regiment's website (thercr.ca). Return to the S17 and head north towards Volturara and San Marco. Both villages sit on the high points of the ridgelines and offer extraordinary views out over the countryside. The

The Church on the summit of Atella. [Tara Campbell]

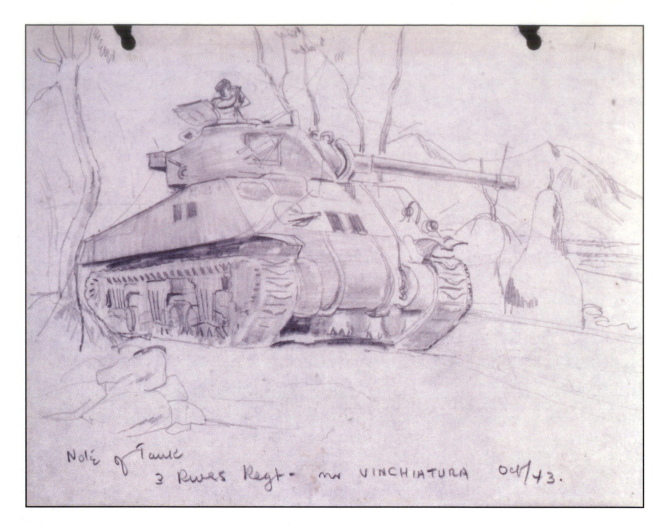

William Ogilvie, *Note of Tank*, *Vinchiaturo*, October 1943 [CWM 19710261-4662].

difficulties facing 1st Brigade's battalions as they sought to evict the enemy holding the San Marco ridge will be immediately apparent.

D Continue to the Fotore River where the Ponte dei 13 Archi ("13 Arch Bridge") spans the valley. The Germans destroyed the centre arches and forced the infantrymen of 3rd Brigade to cross the river under fire on a wide front. The enemy held the high ground in front of the village of Gambatesa until forced to withdraw. You can follow the old S17 across the battlefield before returning to the modern highway which becomes the S645. This is the direct route to Campobasso, but if you prefer to take the road used in 1943 turn left at the S112 to Jelsi where the German defence of the Carapello River cost the West Nova Scotias twenty-seven casualties

before the position could be outflanked. The site is to the south of the village.

E 2nd Brigade then worked its way forward to Vinchiaturo, a village that dominates the main road junction west of Campobasso. This left 1st Brigade with the task of clearing Campobasso, the largest city in the area. Advancing across open ground in front of the hilltop town, the 48th Highlanders met harassing fire, but when the RCRs passed through into Campobasso the enemy was gone.

F Campobasso became "Canada Town" when it was pressed into service as a rest and recreation centre for Canadian troops before and after the bloody struggles at the Moro River and Ortona. There are good hotels in Campobasso to accommodate weary travellers who have followed the Maple Leaf route from Sicily and on through Southern Italy and who are perhaps thinking of continuing to Ortona. The Don Guglielmo and the Cascina Garden are recommended.

(G) The final place of interest on the Southern Italy itinerary is Termoli, less than an hour's drive from Campobasso. This town, where the Three Rivers Regiment won the admiration of the 78th British ("Battleaxe") Division, has beaches, an attractive harbour, and good hotels to attract visitors (the Majestic Molise on the sea coast or the Residenza Sveda in the old town near the harbour are good choices). Sadly, the battlefield where the Three Rivers tanks assisted the 38th (Irish) Brigade in throwing back the German attempts to recapture Termoli has been built over or cleared to make way for the

Autostrada (the A14 carrying traffic along the Adriatic coast). You can still gain some sense of the ground from the German perspective by looking back towards the Autostrada from the SP 168.

From Termoli a short, pleasant drive along the SS 16 takes you to the Sangro River War Cemetery, the starting point of the first tour in our guidebook Ortona and the Liri Valley. Here a whole new stage in the Italian Campaign begins to take shape.

Towed artillery leads a convoy of vehicles as the Canadians push across the Biferno River, west of Campobasso, in late October 1943 [e008300303].

Bari British War Cemetery, located west of the Adriatic port from which it takes its name, is the final resting place for the 210 Canadian soldiers who died during the advance through Southern Italy.

An aerial photo taken in November 1943 showing the crumpled terrain enclosing the Sangro River valley (centre). Here the relatively rapid advance through Southern Italy ended and a much more trying phase of the Italian campaign began. [CWM 19830260-001 #642].

Information

Travel Information

All roads lead through Rome when the destination is Sicily. Air Canada, Air France, and the ever teetering Alitalia currently offer direct flights from Toronto or Montreal to Rome where you can make one of several daily connections to Palermo or Catania. Alitalia (www. alitalia.com – all information is available in English) and Air One (a partner of Lufthansa with a website at www. flyairone.de) are the two choices for domestic flights; but make sure to monitor the day-to-day status of these airlines. Although most foreign carriers flying to Italy use Fiumicino (the Rome airport), some go instead to Malpensa near Milan which also serves as a hub for domestic routes. Several flights to Sicily leave Malpensa each day, but some make a stopover in Rome.

Ferries from Civitavecchia (the port of Rome located fifty kilometres up the coast from the city) present the option of going to Palermo by sea. Other ports in Italy such as Genoa, Naples, or Livorno, also offer ferry service to this destination. Schedules, prices, and bookings can be checked at www.directferries.co.uk. The voyage from Civitavecchia takes twelve hours.

Time, stamina, and nerves of steel permitting, you can drive from Rome to Reggio di Calabria and make the crossing by ferry to Messina. Weigh the pros and cons carefully before you embark on this venture, for the distance is considerable (over 600 kilometres) while the road network around Naples requires close concentration as you plot your course from the A1 (Autostrada del Sole, the same road that runs by Monte Cassino and the Liri Valley battlefields) to the A3 which carries on to the toe of Italy. The Autostradas are toll roads, well maintained, and frequently interspersed with Autogrille stops where you can pause to fortify yourself for the next stage. Portions of the drive take you through regions of great natural beauty and historical interest, but be aware that you will need at least a day and a half to complete the first leg of the journey to Reggio di Calabria where a ferry ride and another knuckle-whitening drive into the interior of Sicily await.

Forewarned is forearmed when driving in Sicilian cities or towns – the lane markers are decorative rather than functional, everyone else has right of way, every second street runs one-way in the direction opposite to the one you want, and pedestrians have the right to cross the road wherever and whenever the spirit moves them. Check the location and route for each hotel or place of interest ahead of time, and establish a good working relationship between driver and navigator.

To supplement the tour maps given in this guidebook, you will want to purchase the Michelin road maps for Sicily (number 432) and for Southern Italy (number 431). The Blue Guide series is another useful resource. In addition to a general guide to Italy, there are Blue Guides focussing on each part of the country, including Sicily and Southern Italy, which put a wealth of practical and cultural information at your disposal.

William Ogilvie, *Air Sentry in a Convoy* [CWM 19710261-4402].

Palermo and Catania, the two airports in Sicily, both have easy and prompt car rental services. Either place makes a convenient starting point for your trip. Arriving in Palermo gives you the opportunity to explore western Sicily as the prelude to your tour of the Canadian battlefields in the central and eastern parts of the island. Sicily is home to the best preserved Greek temples in the world at Segesta and the Valley of the Temples near Agrigento, and the western coast, particularly the lovely town of Erice, is worth a few leisurely days. For Canadians familiar with Normandy, the magnificent Norman monuments in western Sicily – chief among them the three great cathedrals in Palermo, Monreale, and Cefalu – attesting the historical connections between the lands of Canada's two D-Days will be especially compelling. Those wishing to deepen their knowledge of this remarkable period in mediaeval history will find John Julius Norwich's *The Normans in Sicily* (Penguin Books, 1992) an enriching, accessible introduction.

Catania, at the foot of Mount Etna, is well situated for a tour of eastern Sicily, putting you within easy reach of Siracusa or Taormina which rank high among the places you will want to visit. Whether you begin from Palermo or Catania, you can plan your itinerary in such a way that you make Piazza Armerina or the historic citadel of Enna one of your stops. Both make ideal bases from which to embark on a Canadian battlefields tour.

Although *The Canadian Battlefields in Italy* series is intended primarily for travellers setting out on self-directed tours, we hope that the guidebooks will encourage readers, above all students, to take part in the group tours offered by the Canadian Battlefields Foundation and the Gregg Centre at the University of New Brunswick. For information on battlefield tours to Northwest Europe and Italy, go to www.canadianmilitaryhistory.com and look under Study Tours, or visit the Gregg Centre website www.unb.ca/greggcentre/teaching/battlefield_study_tours.html for details about their study tour.

Accommodation

Listed here are the hotels near Piazza Armerina and Regalbuto mentioned in the introduction as the most convenient bases for a tour of the Canadian battlefields in Sicily. We would also strongly recommend staying in Enna, both for the cultural interest of the place and for its proximity to the areas covered in the tours, and therefore we provide addresses for two hotels in the town itself. Advice on hotels in Southern Italy is given in the tour sections covering the itineraries to Potenza and Campobasso. The easiest way to find accommodation in a given place is simply to type the town's name and "hotels" into the Google search engine which will bring up a host of choices. Rather than list hotels in various places, we thought it better to direct readers to a website allowing them to choose from an interesting range of possibilities. While cities or towns like Palermo, Catania, or Siracusa have plenty of good, standard hotels, you may find that a stay in the country brings you closer to the ways and traditions of an older Sicily. Agriturismo.it offers a wide range of accommodation in Sicily featuring old convents, farmhouses, and villas that are often located close to the main centres. Go to the English version at http://en.agriturismo.it and click on the list or the map to get a list of the places available in the Sicilian countryside.

Piazza Armerina

Hotel Mosaici da Battiato
Paratore 8
94015 Piazza Armerina (EN)
tel.:(39) (0)935-685453

Regalbuto

Hotel Castel Miralago
SS 121, km 60
94017 Regalbuto (EN)
tel.: (39) (0)935-72810

Enna

Hotel Sicilia
Piazza Napoleone Colajanni 7
94100 Enna
tel.: (39) (0)935 500488
info@hotelsiciliaenna.it

Hotel Villa Giulia
Via Nazionale Pergusa, 1
94100 Enna
tel.: (39) (0)935 541043

Additional Information

Suggestions for further reading:

Overviews of the Italian Campaign

Carver, Michael. *The Imperial War Museum Book of the War in Italy, 1943-1945. A Vital Contribution to the Victory in Europe.* London: Pan Books, 2002.

Copp, Terry. "Canadian Military History in Perspective," a series of articles on the Italian Campaign in *Legion Magazine,* ongoing from September 2005 – (go to www.legionmagazine.ca and look under "Features" on the menu).

Dancocks, Daniel. *The D-Day Dodgers. The Canadians in Italy, 1943-1945.* Toronto: McClelland and Stewart, 1991.

Graham, Dominick, and Bidwell, Shelford. *Tug of War: The Battle for Italy, 1943-1945.* London: Hodder and Stoughton, 1986.

McAndrew, William. *Canadians and the Italian Campaign, 1943-1945.* Montreal: Art Global Editions, 1996.

Molony, C.J.C. *The Mediterranean and the Middle East,* volumes V and VI, Part 1. London: Her Majesty's Stationery Office, 1973, 1984.

Nicholson, G.W.L. *The Canadians in Italy, 1943-1945.* Official History of the Canadian Army in the Second World War, vol. II. Ottawa: The Queen's Printer, 1956.

Porch, Douglas. *Hitler's Mediterranean Gamble. The North African and the Mediterranean Campaigns in World War II.* London: Weidenfeld and Nicholson, 2004.

Sicily

Barton, Brandey. "Public Opinion and National Prestige: the politics of Canadian Army participation in the invasion of Sicily, 1942-1943," *Canadian Military History* 15/2 (2006), 23-34.

Beattie, Kim. *Dileas. History of the 48th Highlanders of Canada, 1929-1956.* Toronto: 48th Highlanders of Canada, 1957.

Boissonault, C.-M. *Histoire du Royal 22e Régiment.* Quebec: Editions du Pélican, 1964.

Costanzo, Elio. *Sicilia 1943. Breve storia dello sbarco Alleato.* Le Nove Muse Editrice: Catania, 2003.

Delaney, Douglas. *The Soldier's General: Bert Hoffmeister at War.* Vancouver-Toronto: UBC Press, 2005.

D'Este, Carlo. *Bitter Victory. The Battle for Sicily, 1943.* New York: E.P. Dutton, 1988.

Follain, John. *Mussolini's Island. The Battle for Sicily 1943 by the People Who Were There.* Hodder and Stoughton: London, 2005.

Ford, Ken. *Assault on Sicily. Monty and Patton at War.* Sutton Publishing: Phoenix Mill-Thrupp-Stroud, 2007.

Frost, C.S. *Once a Patricia. Memoirs of a Junior Infantry Officer in World War II.* Ottawa: Borealis Press, 2004.

Galloway, Strome. *Bravely into Battle.* Toronto: Stoddart Publishing Company, 1988.

Graham, Howard. *Citizen and Soldier. The Memoirs of Lieutenant-General Howard Graham.* Toronto: McClelland & Stewart, 1987.

Hayes, Geoff. "The Canadians in Sicily: Sixty years on," *Canadian Military History* 12/3 (2003), 5-18.

Johnson, Charles Monroe. *Action with the Seaforths.* New York: Vantage, 1954.

McGeer, Eric. "'Asleep beneath Sicilian skies…' The Canadian War Cemetery at Agira," *Scripta Mediterranea* 24 (2003), 49-66.

Marteinson, John and McNorgan, Michael. *The Royal Canadian Armoured Corps. An Illustrated History.* Toronto: Robin Brass Studio, 2000.

Mowat, Farley. *The Regiment.* Toronto: McClelland & Stewart Limited, 1955.